CW01651708

To the memory of my father
Egon Kirk Dupont

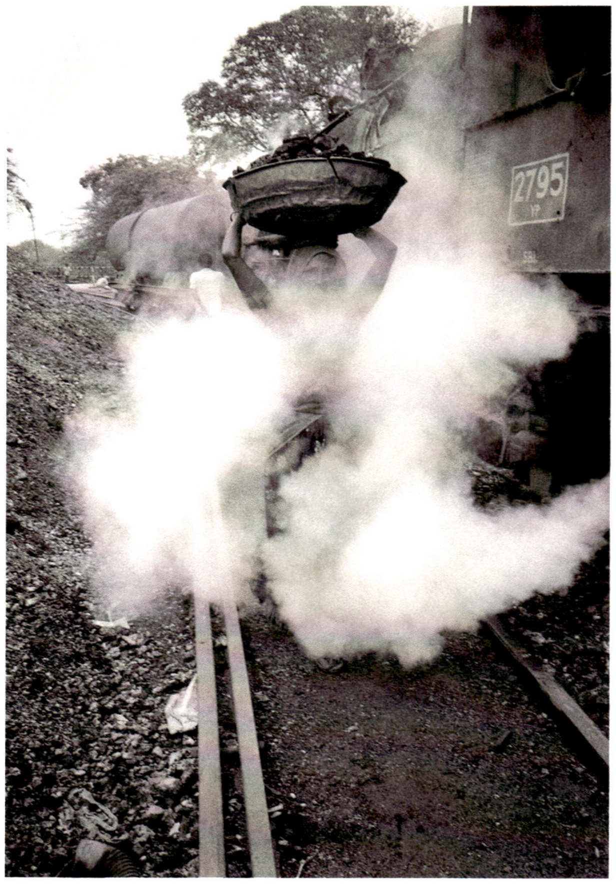

Collecting used coal for recycling
Rana Pratap Nagar, Rajastan.

STEAM

India's last steam trains

photographs by
Stephen Dupont

introduction by
Mark Tully

DEWI LEWIS
PUBLISHING

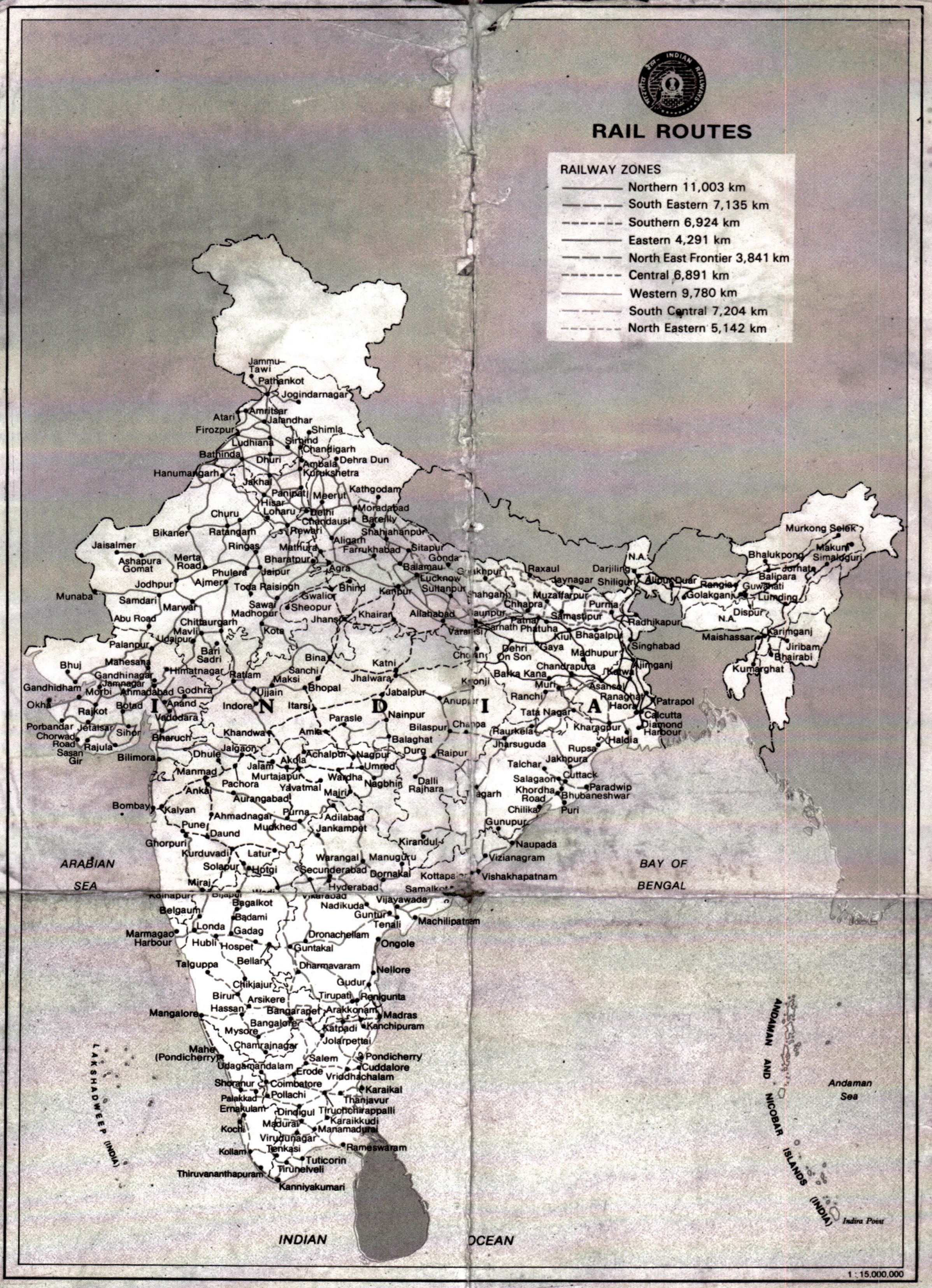
RAIL ROUTES
RAILWAY ZONES
Northern 11,003 km
South Eastern 7,135 km
Southern 6,924 km
Eastern 4,291 km
North East Frontier 3,841 km
Central 6,891 km
Western 9,780 km
South Central 7,204 km
North Eastern 5,142 km
I N D I A
ARABIAN SEA
BAY OF BENGAL
INDIAN OCEAN
Andaman Sea
LAKSHADWEEP (INDIA)
ANDAMAN AND NICOBAR ISLANDS (INDIA)
Indira Point
1 : 15,000,000

Steam

Mark Tully

The arrival of the steam locomotive in India was delayed, so too was its departure. Speculators, certain that there were lucrative investments to be made building railways in India, were kept at bay for several years by complicated, cumbersome, consultations between the three heads of the ruling behemoth – the Governor General in Calcutta, and in London, The Court of the East India Company and the Government of the day. So it wasn't until April 16th 1853, twenty three years after the opening of the Liverpool Manchester railway, that a grandiose starting pistol, a 21-gun salute, fired off the inaugural train from Bombay to Thana, a distance of 21 miles. There was plenty of contradictory advice, and conflicting pressures too, when it came to ending the steam era. Although the Railway Board has been announcing the demise of steam since the 1980s I heard the haunting sound of a whistle at the mainline junction of Ratlam last year.

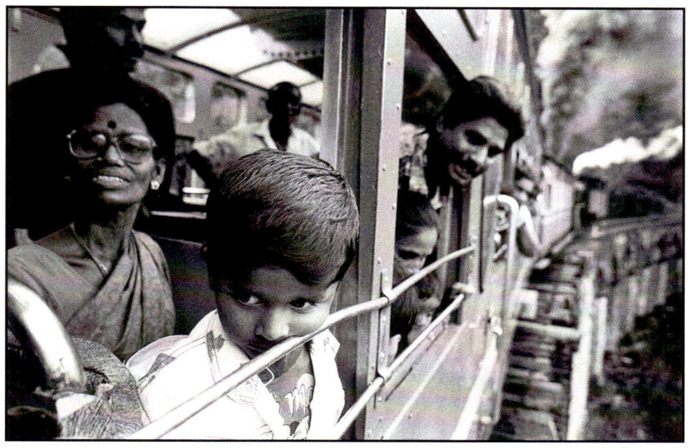

Nilgiri Express, Tamil Nadu

The ICS, or Indian Civil Service, claimed to be 'the steel frame' which held the Raj together, but for my money it was the railways which deserved that title. Some have even argued that the British were the sole beneficiaries of the railways they built. Steam hauled trains did transport soldiers to defend the North West Frontier and to the cantonments within India where they overawed the subject people. Steam powered the freight trains, which killed India's traditional textile industry, taking cotton from previously inaccessible parts of the country to the ports where it was exported as raw material for the Lancashire mills. Hopes were frequently expressed that steam locomotives would prove powerful enough to carry the message of Christianity to all corners of India, but in this they proved less successful.

In serving their British masters, however, steam engines also transformed the lives of Indians. Restrictions of caste were temporarily set aside as Indians crowded into smoke-filled carriages to have a darshan, or sight, of distant Gods they would never have been able to reach by the roads of those times. They poured into the cities that the railways created too, in search of work. Steam freight trains did reduce the cost of food in areas which did not grow enough for themselves and special railways were built to carry food to areas notorious for famines – areas that couldn't be reached by carts pulled by bullocks which within fifty miles had consumed more grain than they carried.

Trains required timetables and although they didn't make punctuality an Indian virtue they did, as in Britain, introduce the first standard time. Indian railways had a twenty four clock from the earliest days of timetables. It had to be twenty-four hours otherwise late running over long distances would have caused hopeless confusion. As it was during the Second War my Uncle once reprimanded a station master for allowing the Madras Mail to leave early, only to be told that the train he thought he'd missed was yesterday's.

Although steam traction under the Raj never reached the speed or sophistication of the best that Britain achieved, experts were sent out from time to time to see what improvements could be made in the way the Raj ran the railways. The Robertson report of 1903 fell foul of the haughty Lord Curzon, who thought it a shoddy piece of work and confiscated the hapless author's steamer ticket home until he did a better job. But I doubt whether even Lord Curzon would have dared to condescend to Sir William Stanier, designer of the magnificent Duchesses of the London Midland and Scottish Railway, when he came to India in 1938 to look into the problems of a class of locomotives aimed to standardise motive power. The locomotives failed to deliver the promised power and had an unfortunate tendency to derail. Even after the modifications that Sir William proposed their safety was suspect and their speed consequently limited.

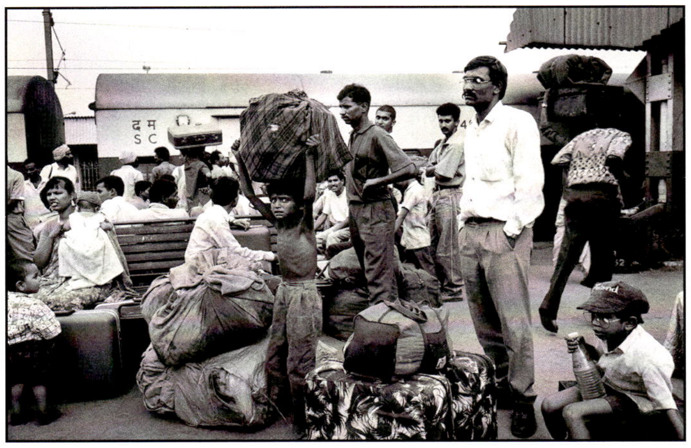
A boy struggles with a heavy load. New Delhi Station

From the very first days Indian railways underestimated the demand for their services. One way round this, they found, was to cram many more third class passengers into their carriages than they could carry with any degree of comfort. The facilities provided were deplorable too. Lack of lavatories on trains was a particular problem leading one distressed passenger to complain in a letter to the East India Railway 'I am arrive by passenger train at Ahmedpore Station and my belly is too much swelling with Jack Fruit. I am therefore went to privy. Just as I am doing the nuisance, that guard making whistle blow for train to go off and I am running with lotah (brass pot) in one hand and dhotie in the next when I am fall over and expose my shockings to man and female on the platform.'[1] First and second class passengers were provided with Waiting Rooms, third class with appropriately named Sheds, if lucky.

The supply of freight wagons exceeded demand too, so that railway staff imposed rationing to their own advantage. Wagons would suddenly become available after payment of a suitable sum to the local station master. Those who didn't pay were likely to find their wagons uncoupled in the middle of nowhere because of a mysterious mechanical fault. If they wanted to consign foodstuffs they would be given wagons that had been used for conveying such malodorous cargos as kerosene or tar. Corruption was also rife on passenger services, where ticket inspectors were only too happy to strike a bargain with ticketless travellers. Often tickets could only be purchased through the intervention of touts. In 1937 one of those many committees which studied the working of the railways reported that corruption was 'endemic'.

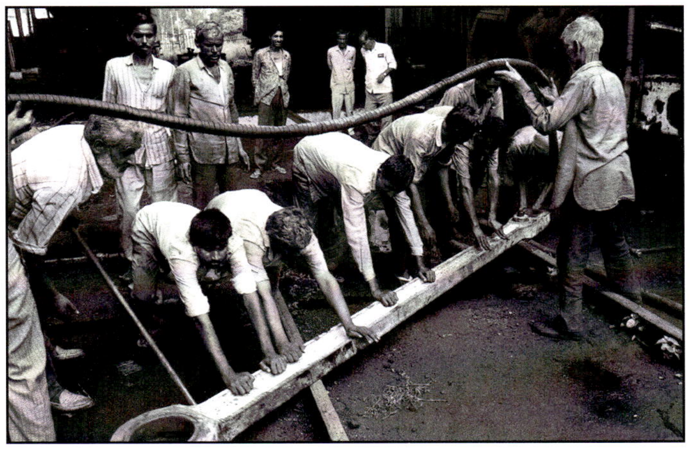

Repairing an engine, Laksa loco shed, Uttar Pradesh

Freight traffic was slow – often travelling at an average speed of just 4 m.p.h. – and was made even slower in some cases by the need to trans-ship from meter gauge to broad gauge. Lord Dalhousie, the Governor General who pioneered Indian railways had experienced the war of the gauges in Britain, and he warned against a repetition of that mistake in India. But within seven years of his laying down office it was repeated, and the consequences survive to this day. Passenger trains varied from the very slow to the not very fast. Even the poshest passengers arriving at Bombay on the weekly P&O liner service and travelling on to Calcutta faced a journey of 37 hours, at an average speed of 36 mph, on the prestigious Imperial Mail.

During the Second War the steel frame, rusted from lack of maintenance, strained by the pressure of troop and military supply movements, still just held, but only just. Jawaharlal Nehru the first Prime Minister of independent India complained that he had inherited a railway system 'in an obnoxious state.' He went on to say 'I would not have believed it if I had not seen it myself, how many people were jammed into our third class compartments specially and to some extent in the other classes too. So far as goods were concerned I believe mountains of them piled up in our ports'. Partition compounded the problems, cutting off India's routes to Assam in the North East and Kashmir in the North West, leaving workshops on the wrong side of the border, and gaping holes in the locomen's rostas which had been dominated by Muslims. But somehow the railways kept going. In Punjab, although trains were attacked by Sikh and Hindu marauders on one side and Muslims on the other, they transported 700,000 refugees in one month across the border which was baptised with blood. Three thousand Muslim passengers were massacred in just one incident.

After the trauma of partition Indian railways started to plan for the new priorities of an independent nation. It was clear that there would be no decrease in demand, rather an increase was to be expected with Nehru's ambitious plans to industrialise India and the prosperity everyone hoped was just round the corner. One answer would have been early retirement for steam, but drastic solutions are alien to India, and so it wasn't until the mid fifties that the railways turned their attention to diesel and electric traction. They could at least narrow the gap between supply and demand by hauling longer trains faster. Even then the railways decided to proceed cautiously. Nehru, and indeed his daughter Indira Gandhi, dreamt of a self-sufficient India. They believed in pulling the economy up by its bootstraps. To replace steam rapidly would have required importing diesels and strangling India's plans to manufacture its own locomotives at birth. At the same time India had plenty of coal but was short of oil. In the long run this policy has succeeded because India is now one of the largest manufacturers of diesel and electric locomotives in the world.

It isn't only motive power which has changed gradually on Indian railways. The shadow of the Raj has not lifted. A web of red-tape, still spreads from Railway Headquarters in Delhi out to the remotest station master. The foreman trying to keep Ratlam going – one of the last steam sheds – complained to me that his superior officers in the engineering branch were 'nothing more than technical clerks'. 'All they do', he said 'is tell you that you can't have the spare parts you need.' Although the sale of tickets is computerised at the main stations passengers are still required to fill in a form, which includes entering their age. The bureaucratic checks and balances remain in place but they are no more successful in curbing corruption than they were when they were instituted during the Raj.

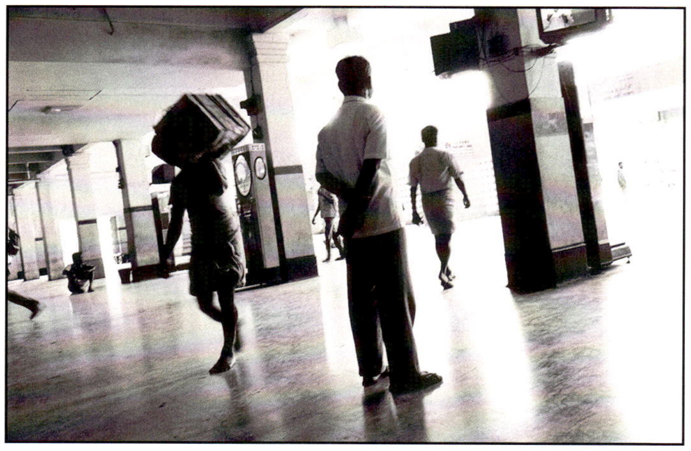

Madurai Station, Tamil Nadu

The British were renowned for their lavish use of labour. In my parents' house in Calcutta we had fifteen servants, each with a minutely defined responsibility – job demarcation of a highly sophisticated order. The railways followed this tradition and still do. With one and a half million staff they have probably the largest payroll in the world. They employ seven times more manpower per route kilometre than most European railways. They are now committed to cutting staff by two percent per year, but there's no sign of the drastic down-sizing that Western management consultants would advocate. Indian railways will have nothing to do with them. In 1997 M.Ravindra, the Chairman of the Railway Board, made that clear when he told me 'We have managed change over the last twenty years without the help of those smart alecs'.

The attitude of passengers hasn't changed from the days of the Raj either. The railways were then seen as the most potent emblem of Imperial rule and so were the obvious target for the independence movement. Although they now have independence, Indians continue to take out their grievances against their government on the railways. Sitting on tracks, burning carriages, and stoning trains are still among the most common forms of protest in this turbulent democracy. The Railways have mounted many campaigns to persuade Indians to regard trains as their own, and so treat them with respect, but the passenger who removed a mirror from a lavatory and then scrawled on the wall, *Railway property is public property and I've taken my share*, remains all too typical.

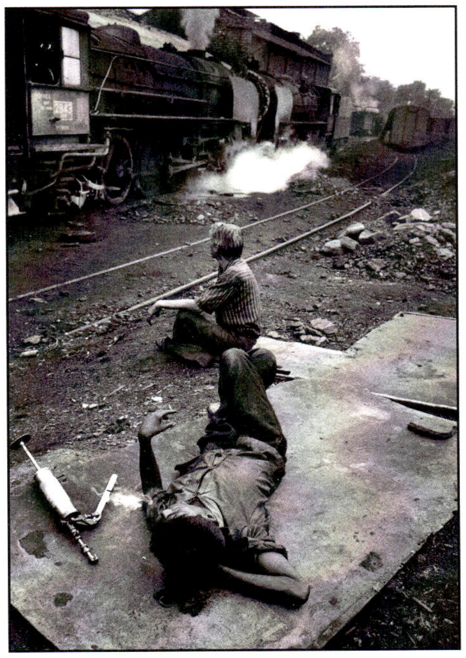

Bidi break at Rana Pratap loco shed, Rajustan

With passengers who feel free to do what they like with their railways, staff who resist all changes, and politicians who put politics before commercial common sense, it's remarkable that the railways have made any progress since Independence. But progress there has been. Unlike most railways, India's passenger and freight traffic has increased consistently over the last fifty years and they now carry six million people per day. New lines have been opened. The British left the West Coast without a railway and that gap has just been filled. There is even a plan to tunnel through the mountains and connect the Kashmir valley with the railway network. Many meter gauge lines have now been converted to broad gauge, which would have delighted Lord Dalhousie.

The long lingering death of steam, and that shadow of the Raj over the railways, suit a country which has always resisted sudden change. There couldn't be a butcher like Dr Beeching in India, whose civilization has survived for thousands of years because it has never hurried. It's absorbed new ideas. It's adapted to development. It's preserved what is best in the old. Joginder Singh who drove one of the last steam expresses on the broad gauge, often enduring temperatures of more than 50 degrees on the footplate, told me with pride 'There's nothing to diesel, you can be a master in a few weeks. After twenty years I was still not a master of steam.' He wouldn't have been an Indian if he hadn't respected his past. So it's no surprise that steam survived so long in India, and even now it isn't going to disappear entirely. It's to be preserved on two of the hill railways which would have been closed long ago as hopelessly uncommercial in countries with less respect for their past.

1. Quoted in *Railways of the Raj* by Michael Satow and Ray Desmond, Scolar Press, London, 1980.

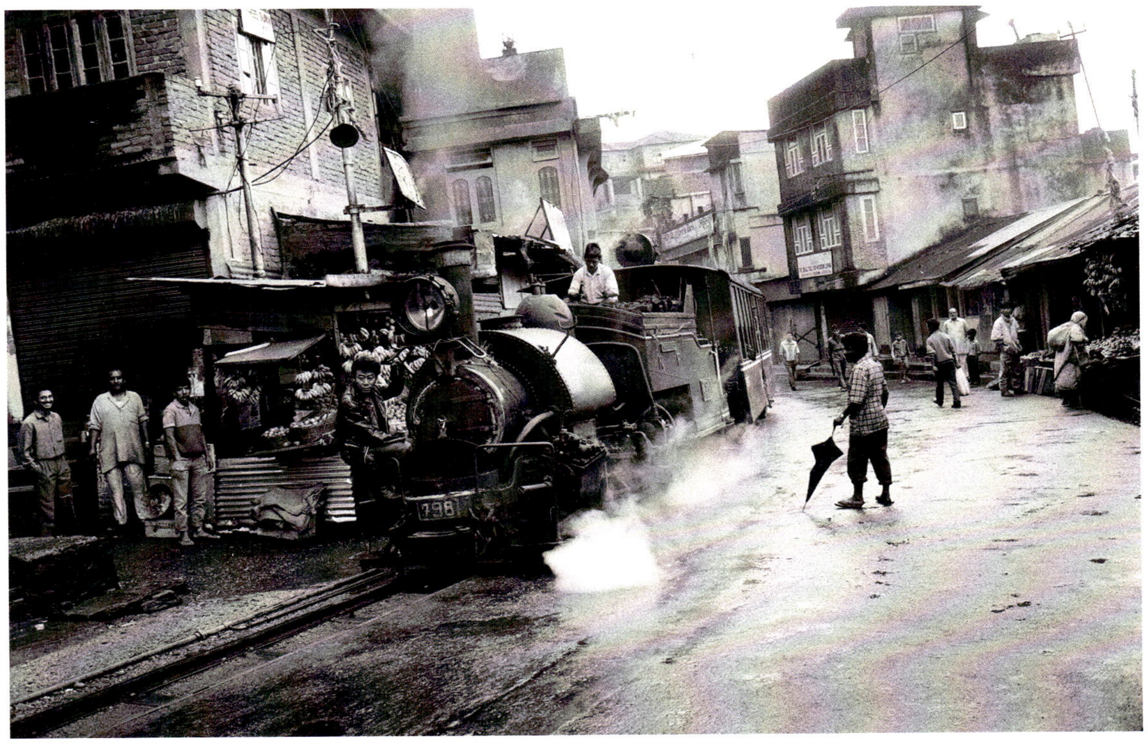

The 'toy train' near Darjeeling, West Bengal.

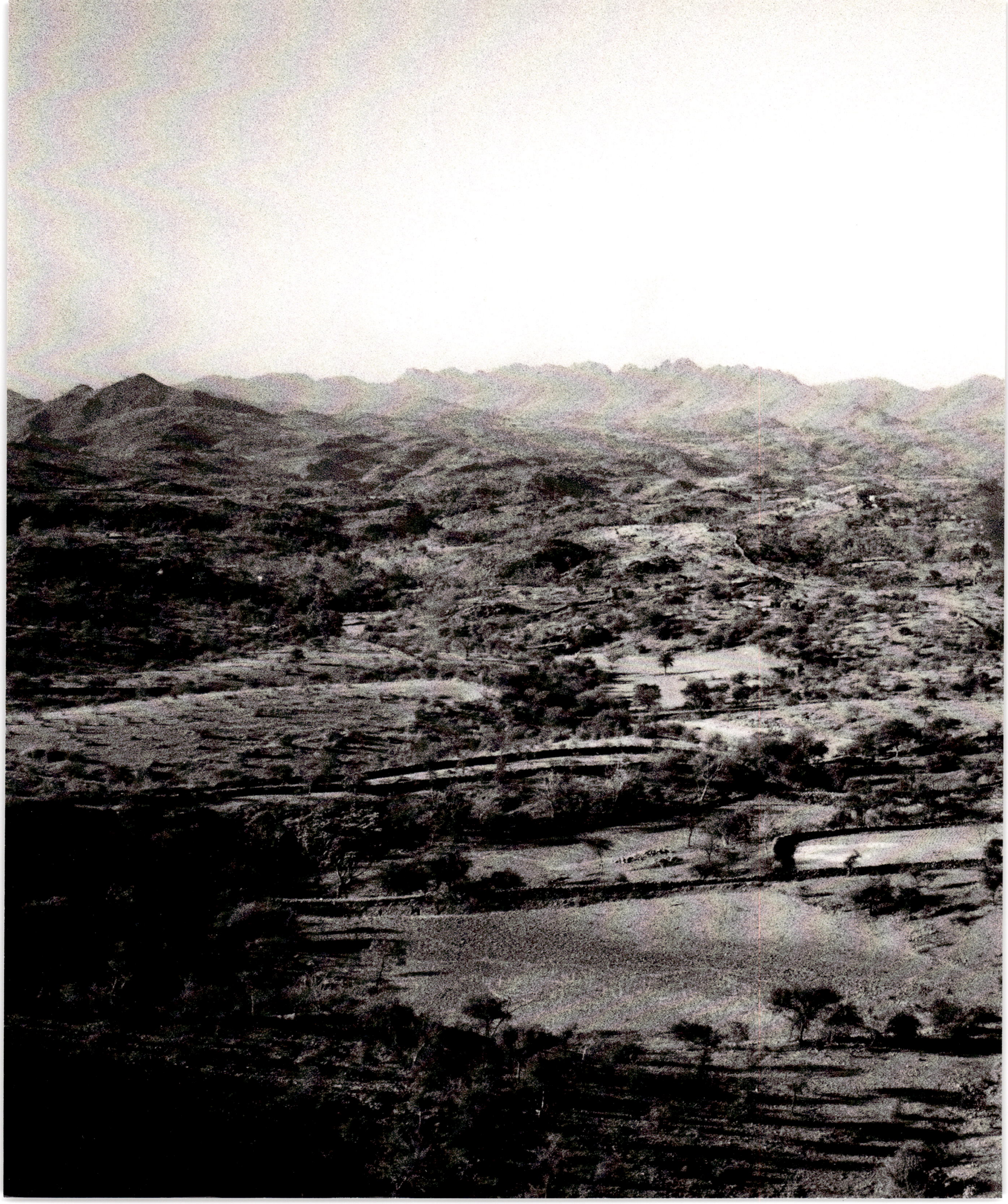

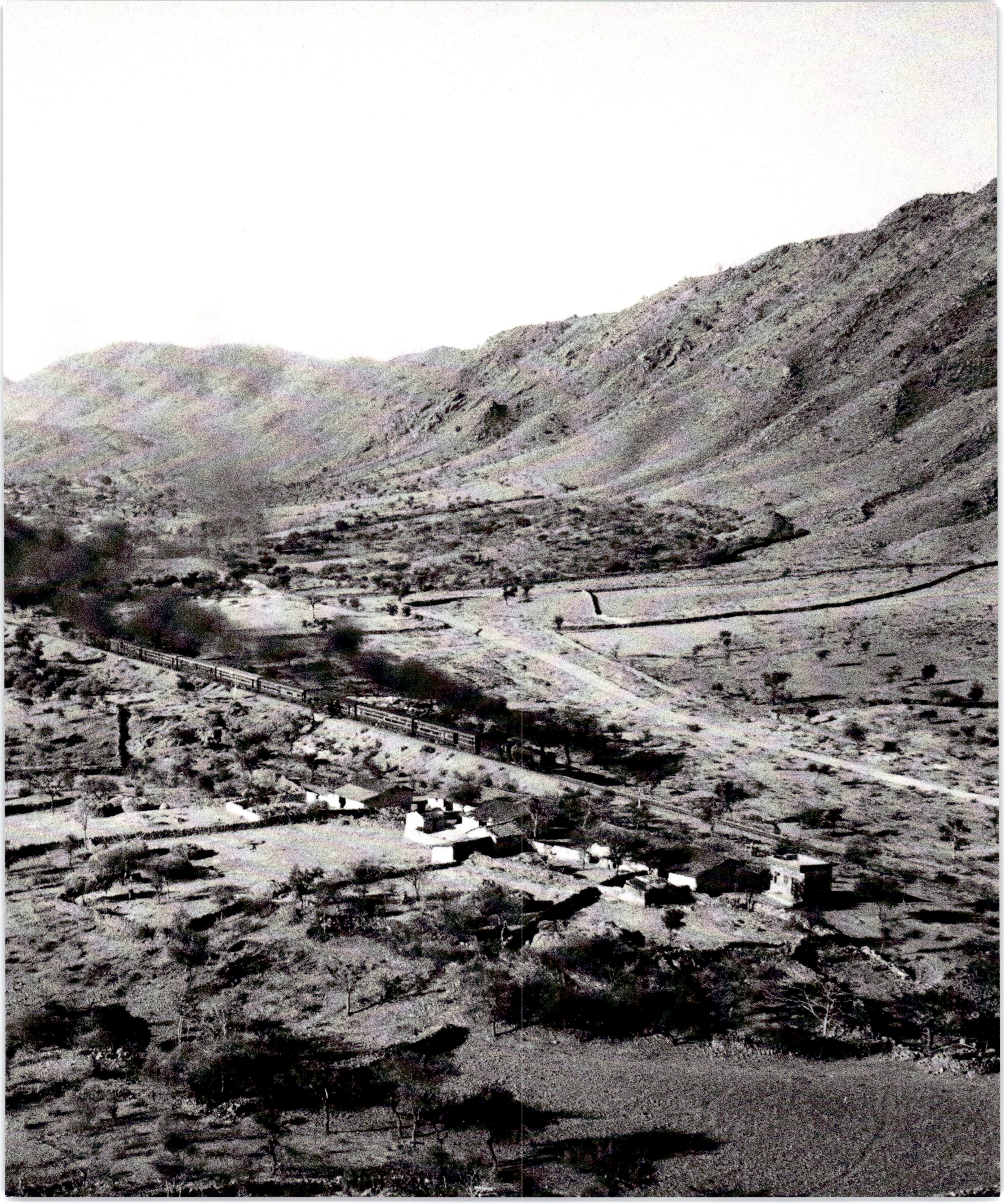

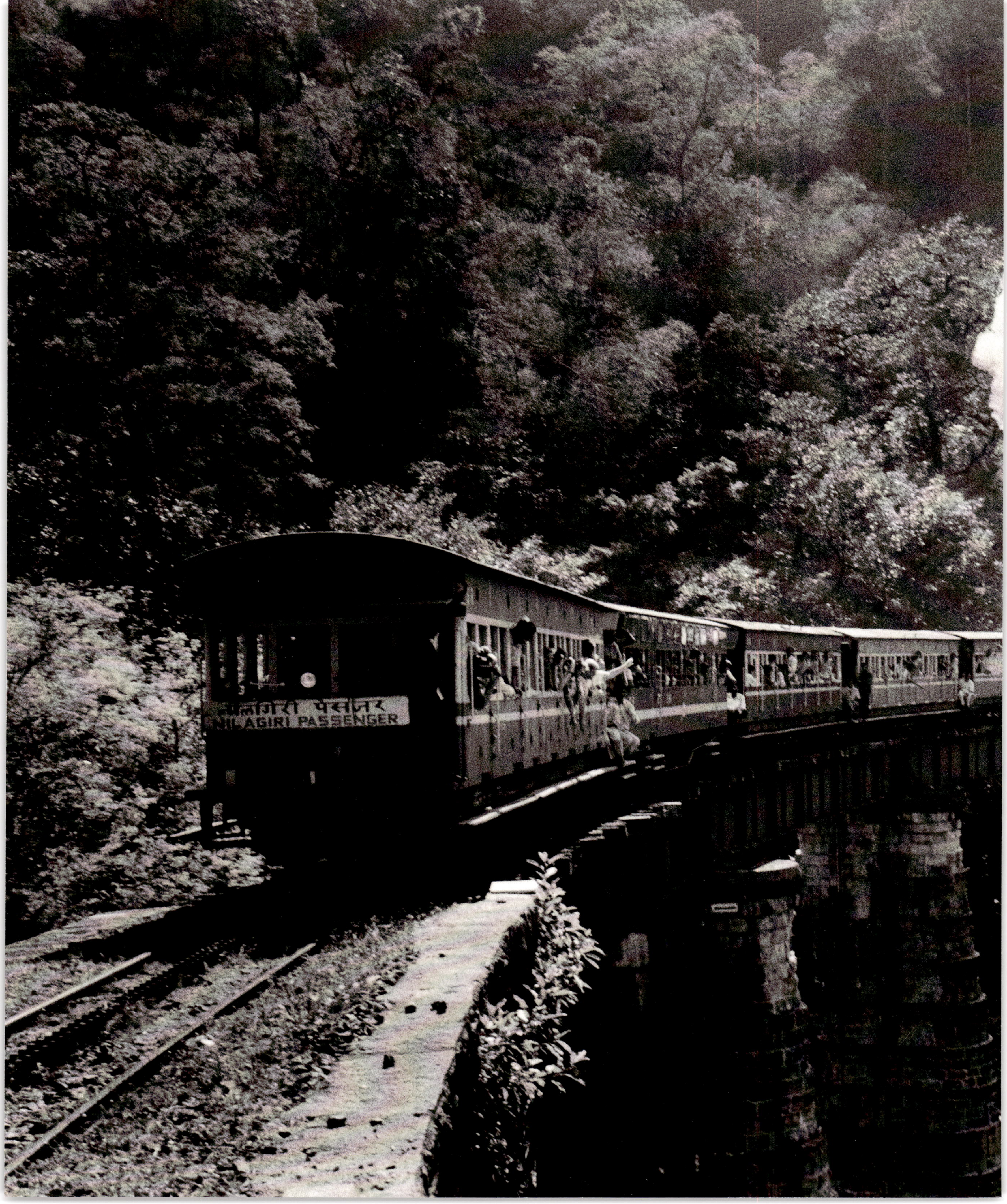
NILAGIRI PASSENGER

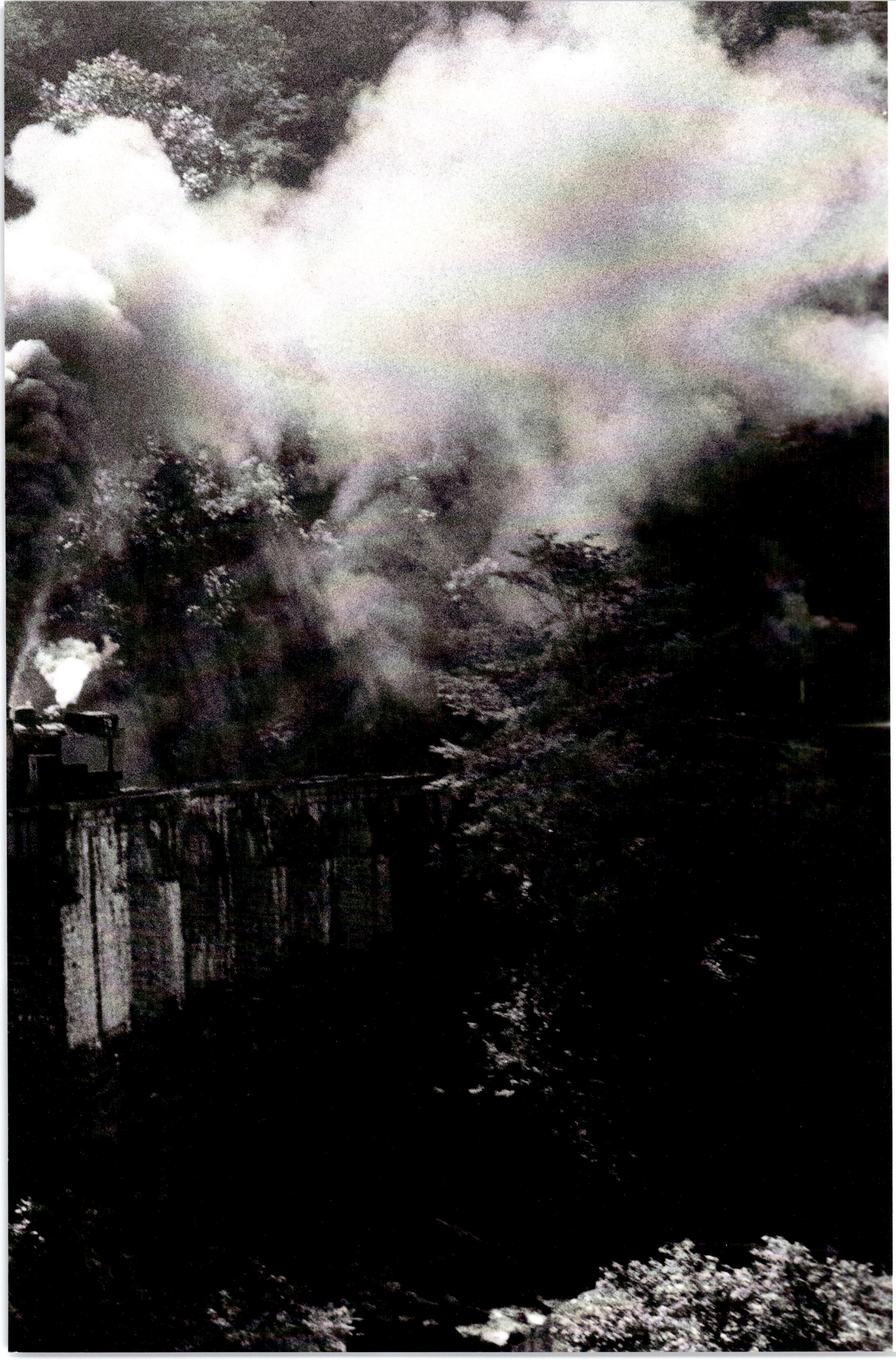

previous page
Steam train
just outside
Udaipur,
Rajastan.

The Nilgiri Hills,
Tamil Nadu.

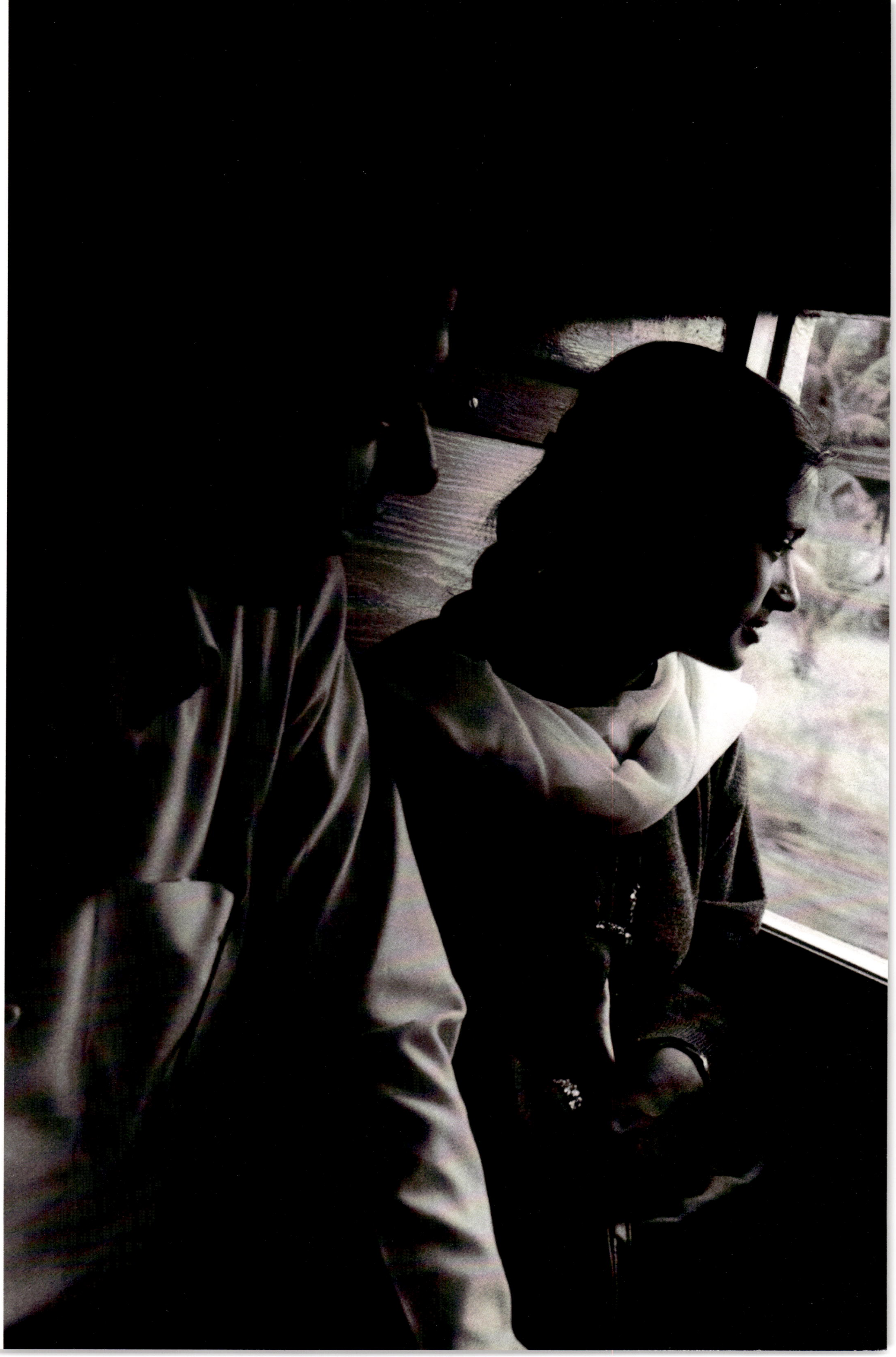

Passengers on
the Nilgiri Express,
Tamil Nadu.

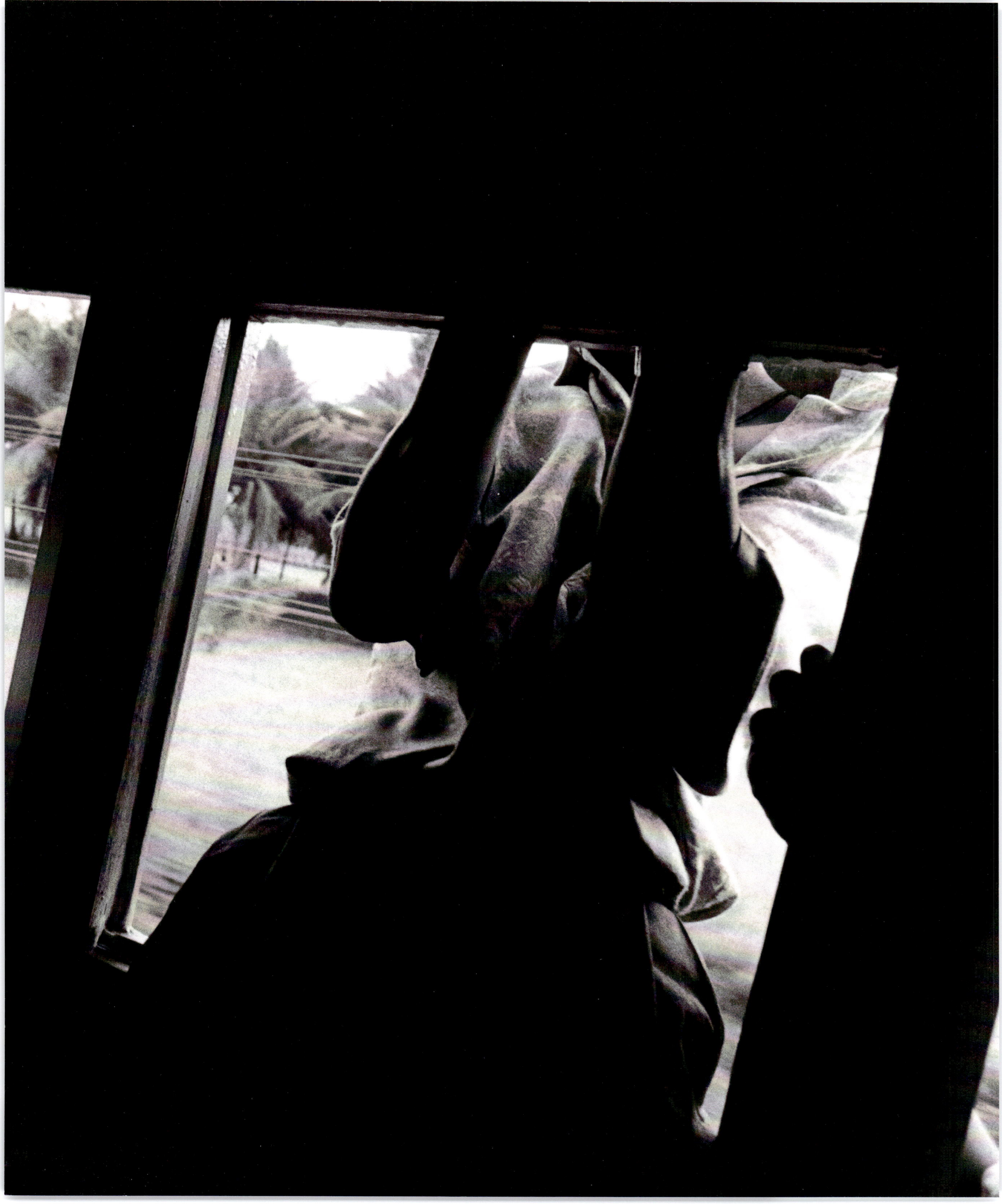

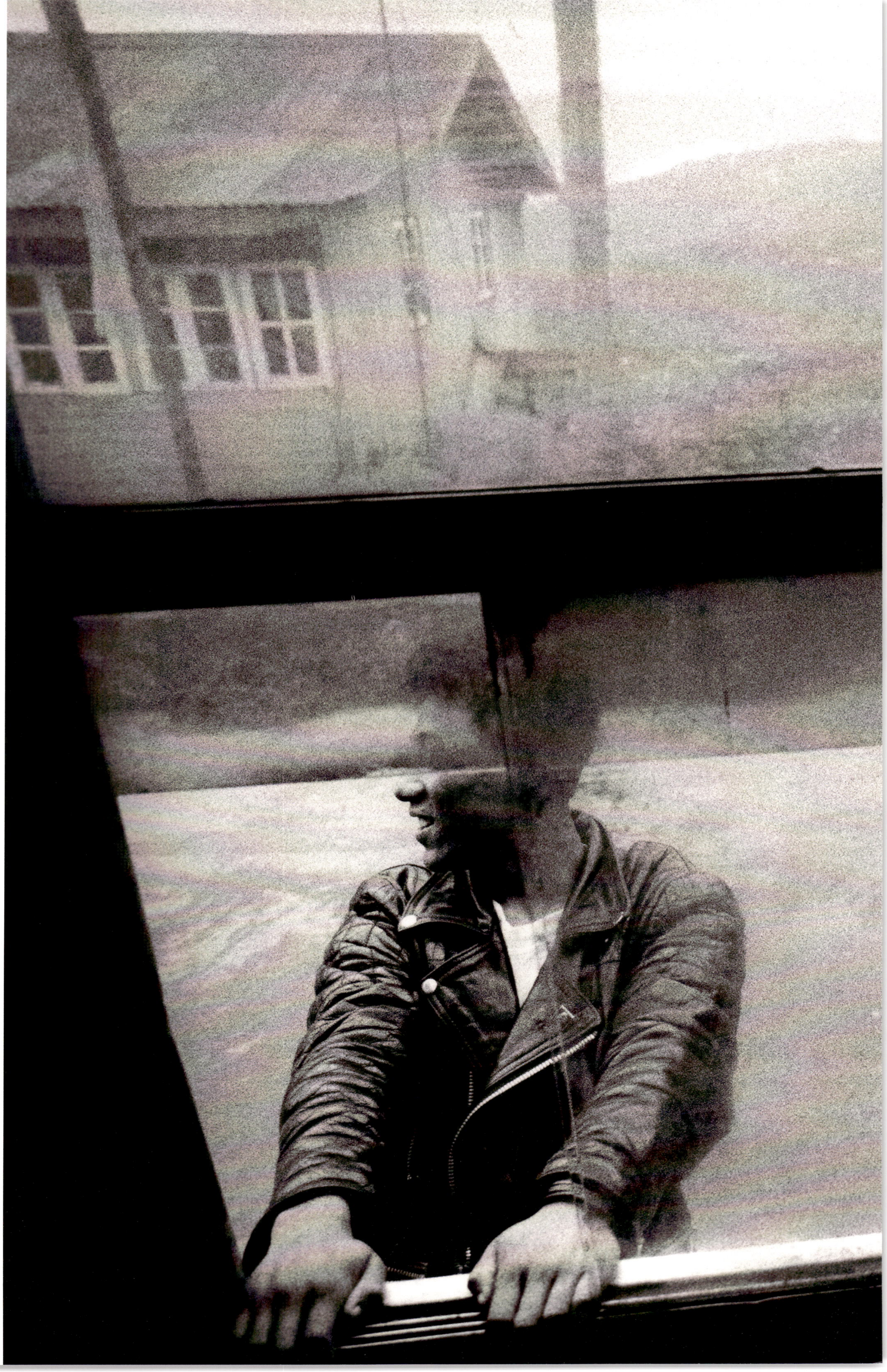

Locals riding
the Darjeeling
'toy train',
West Bengal.

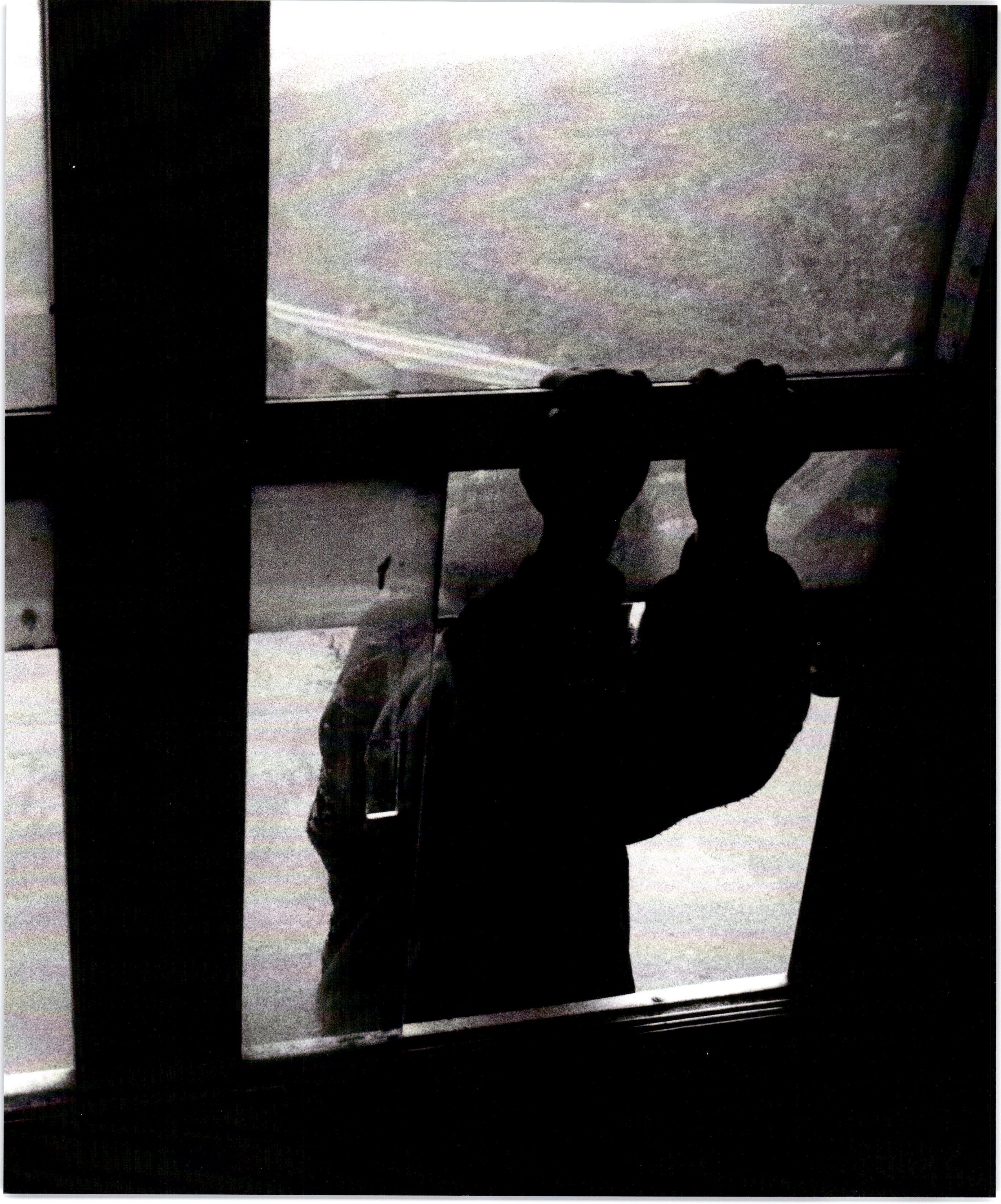

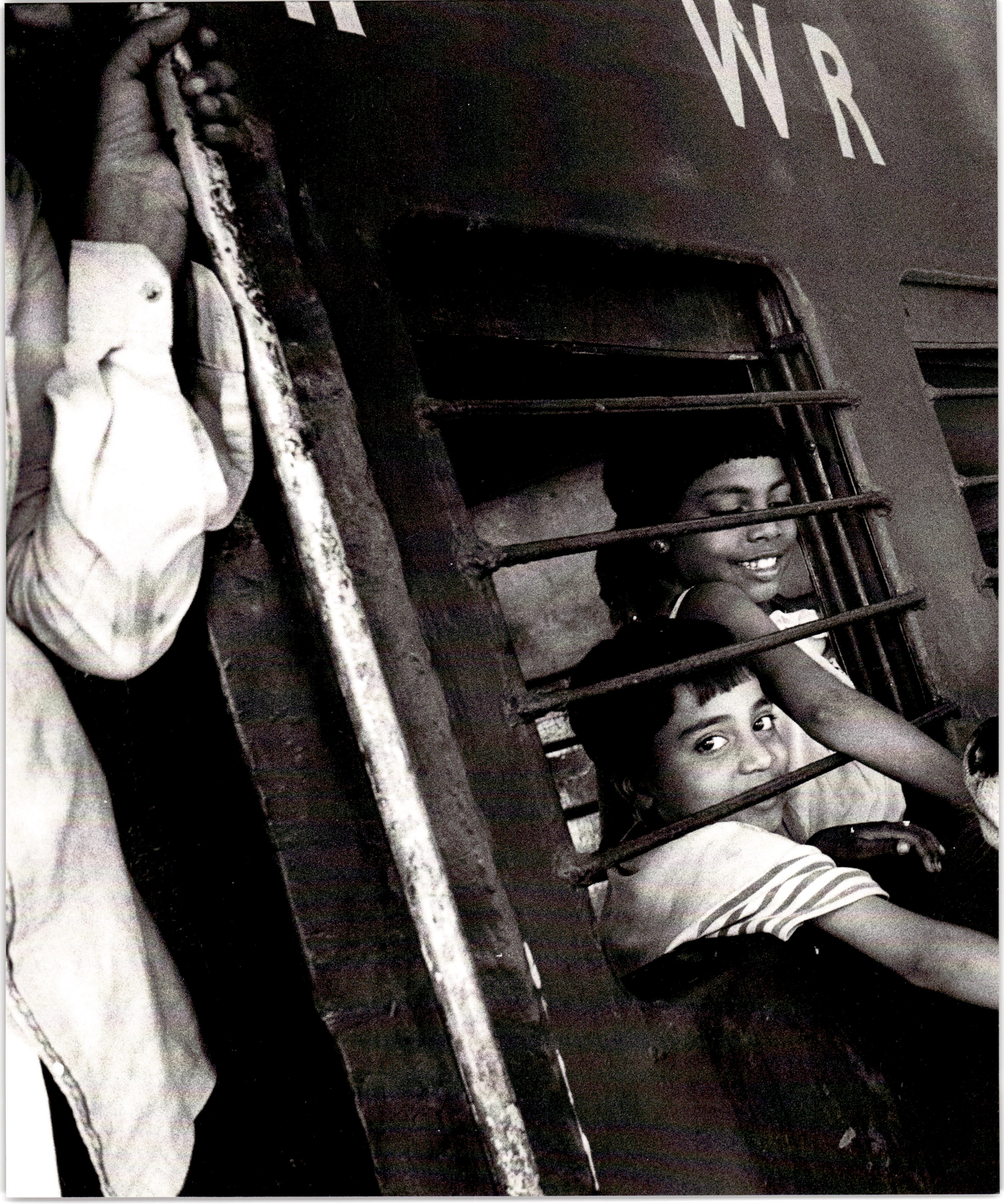
WR

following page
The Darjeeling
'toy train',
West Bengal.

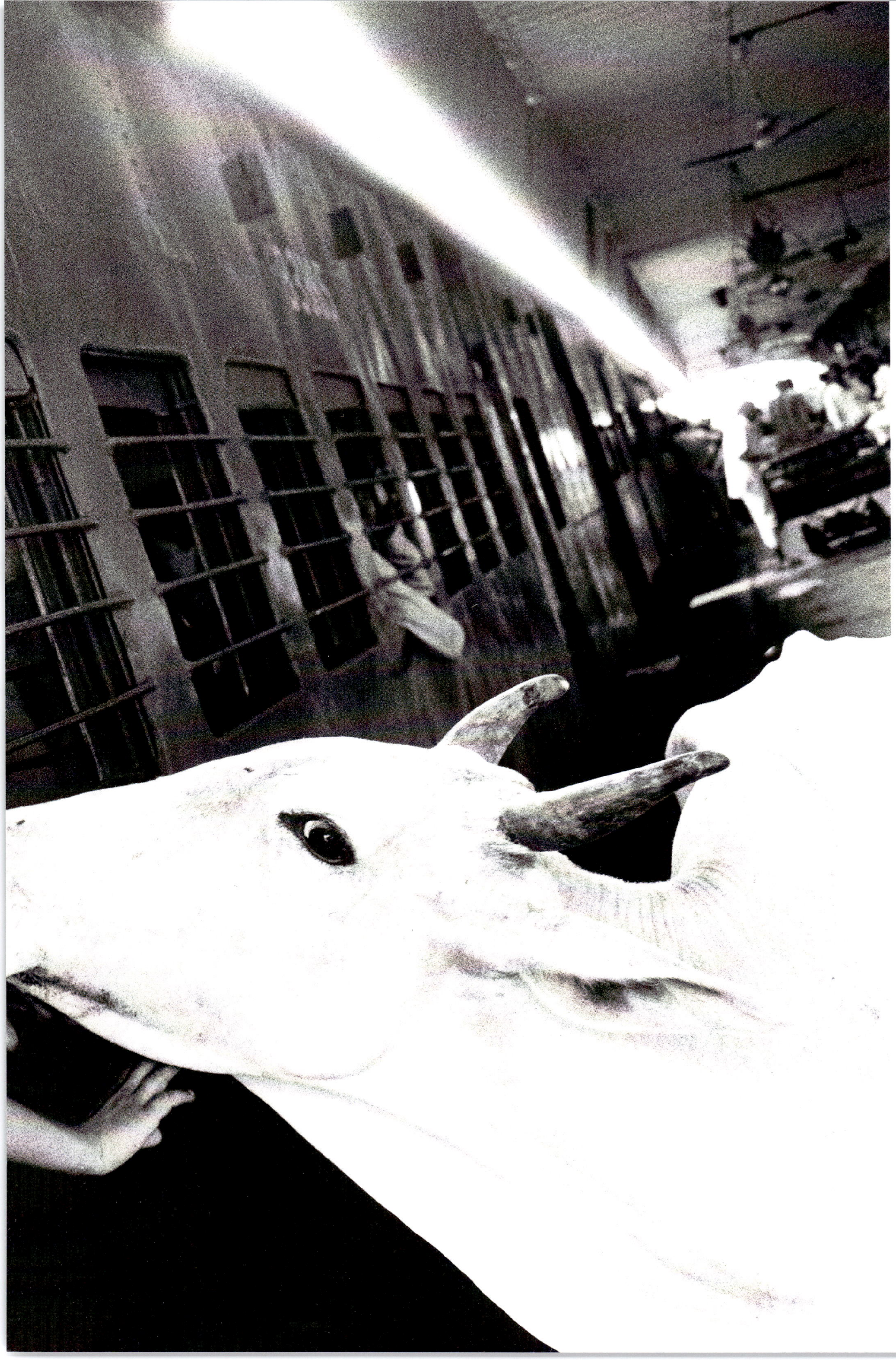

Mavli Junction,
Rajastan.

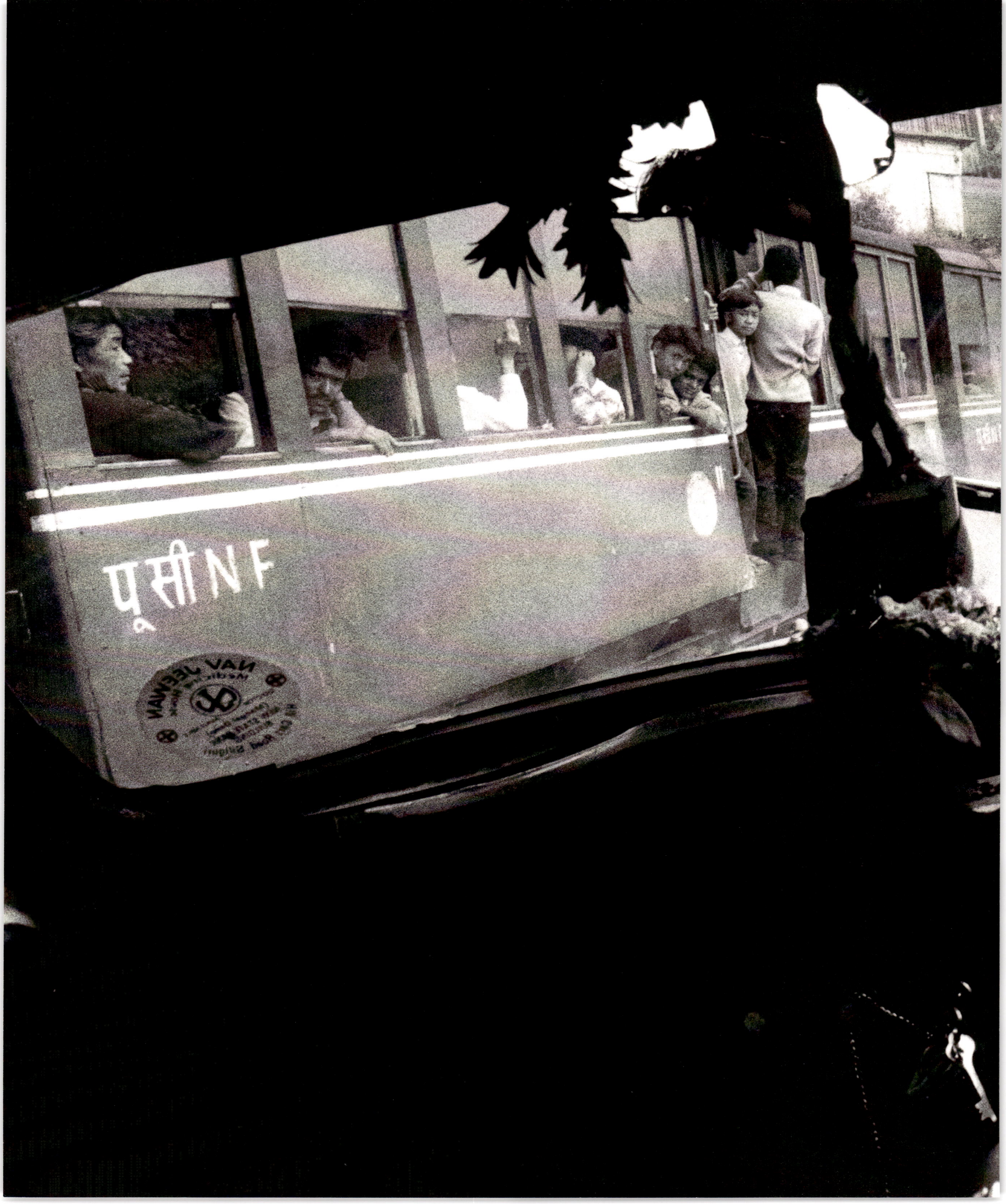
पूसी NF
NAV JEEWAN

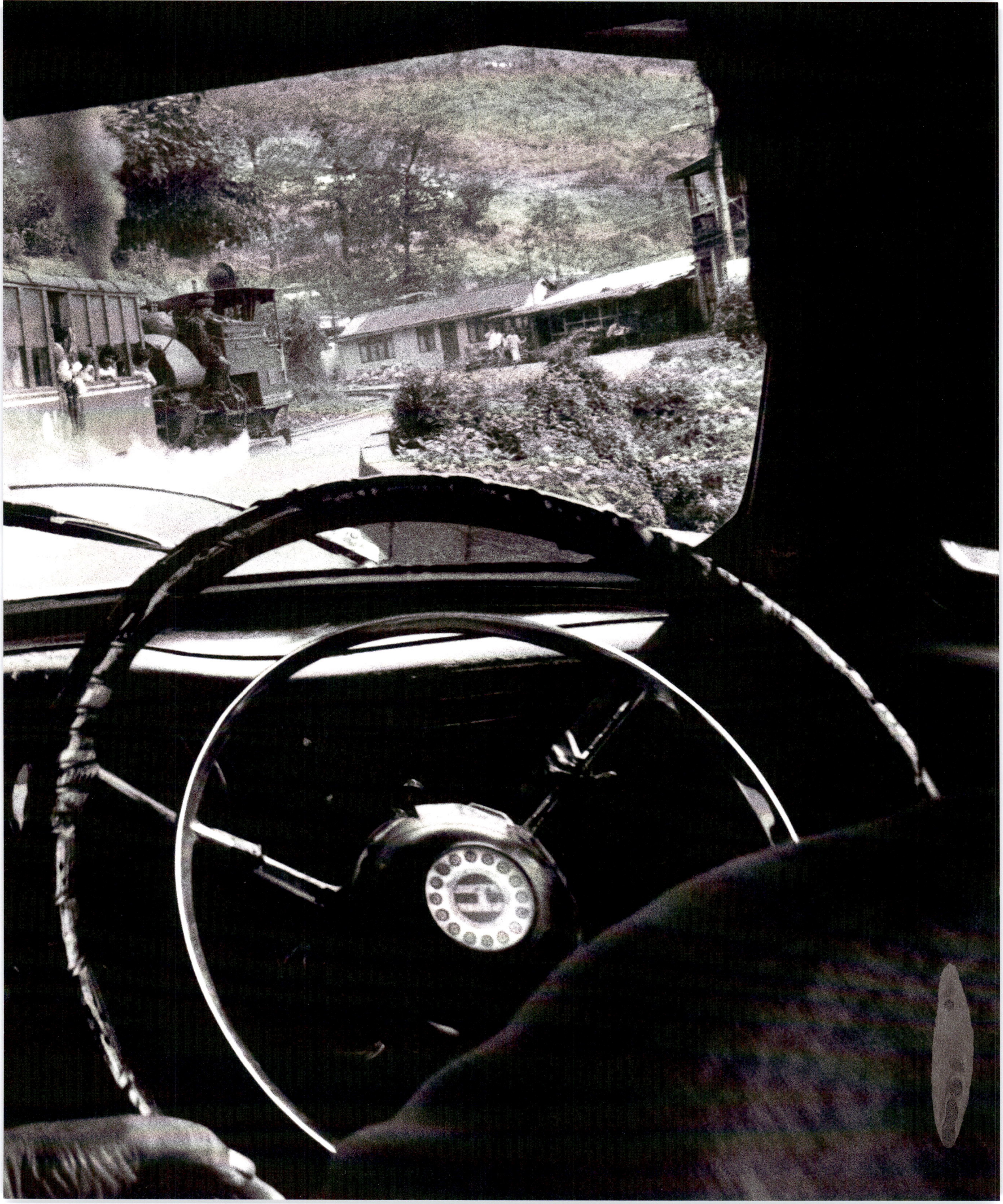

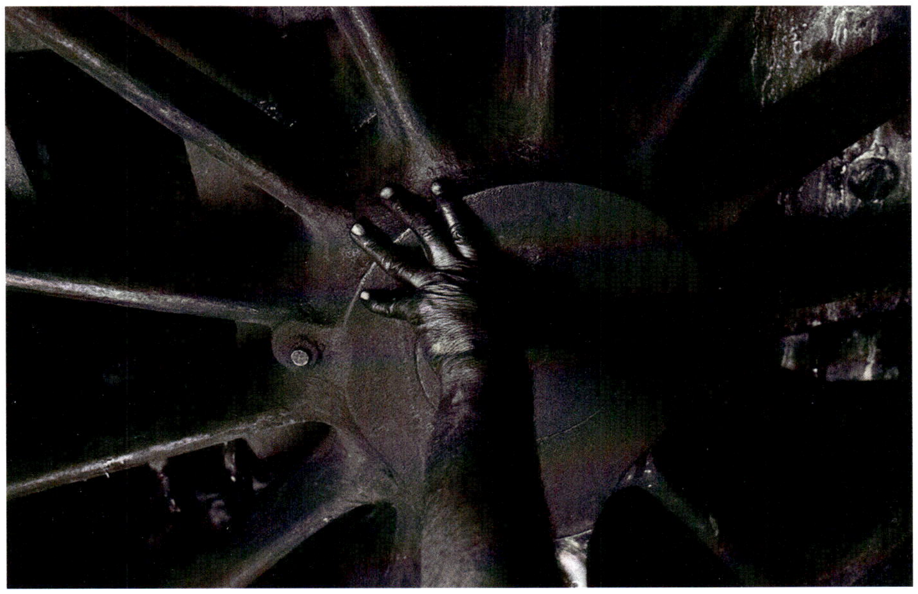

Sabarati steam loco shed, Gujarat.

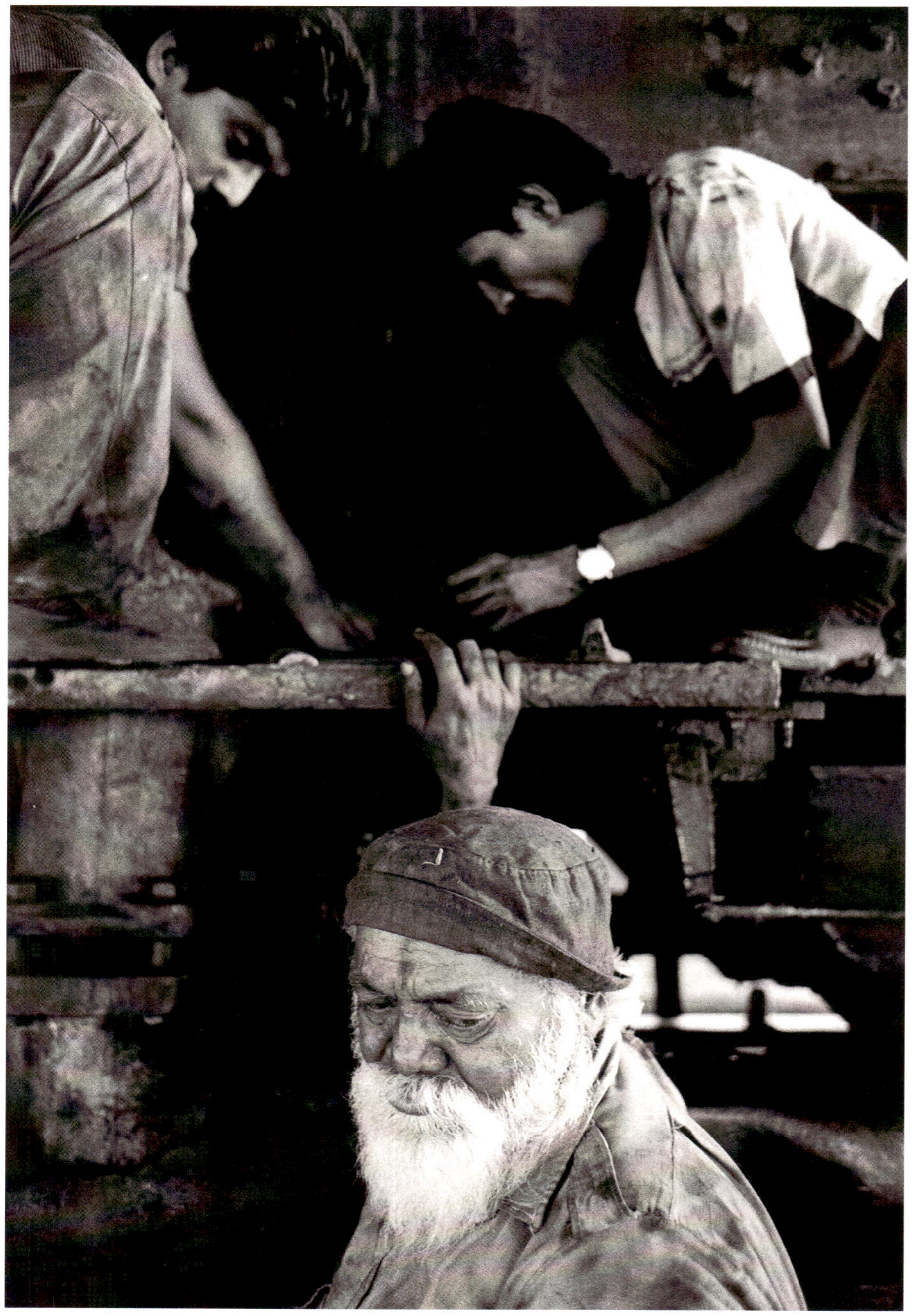

Workers at Sabarati steam loco shed, Gujarat.

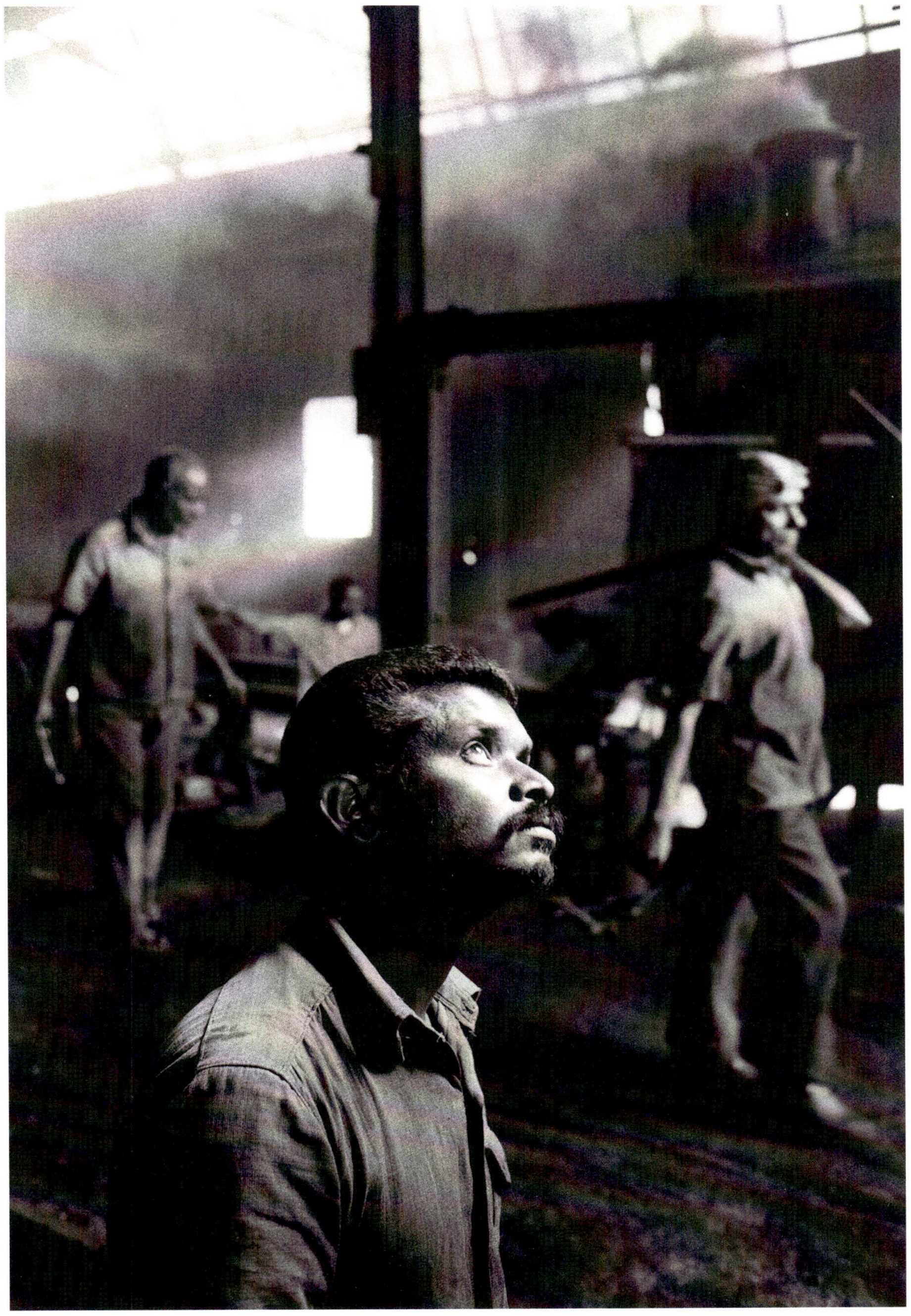

Workers at Coonoor steam loco shed, Nilgiri Hills, Tamil Nadu.

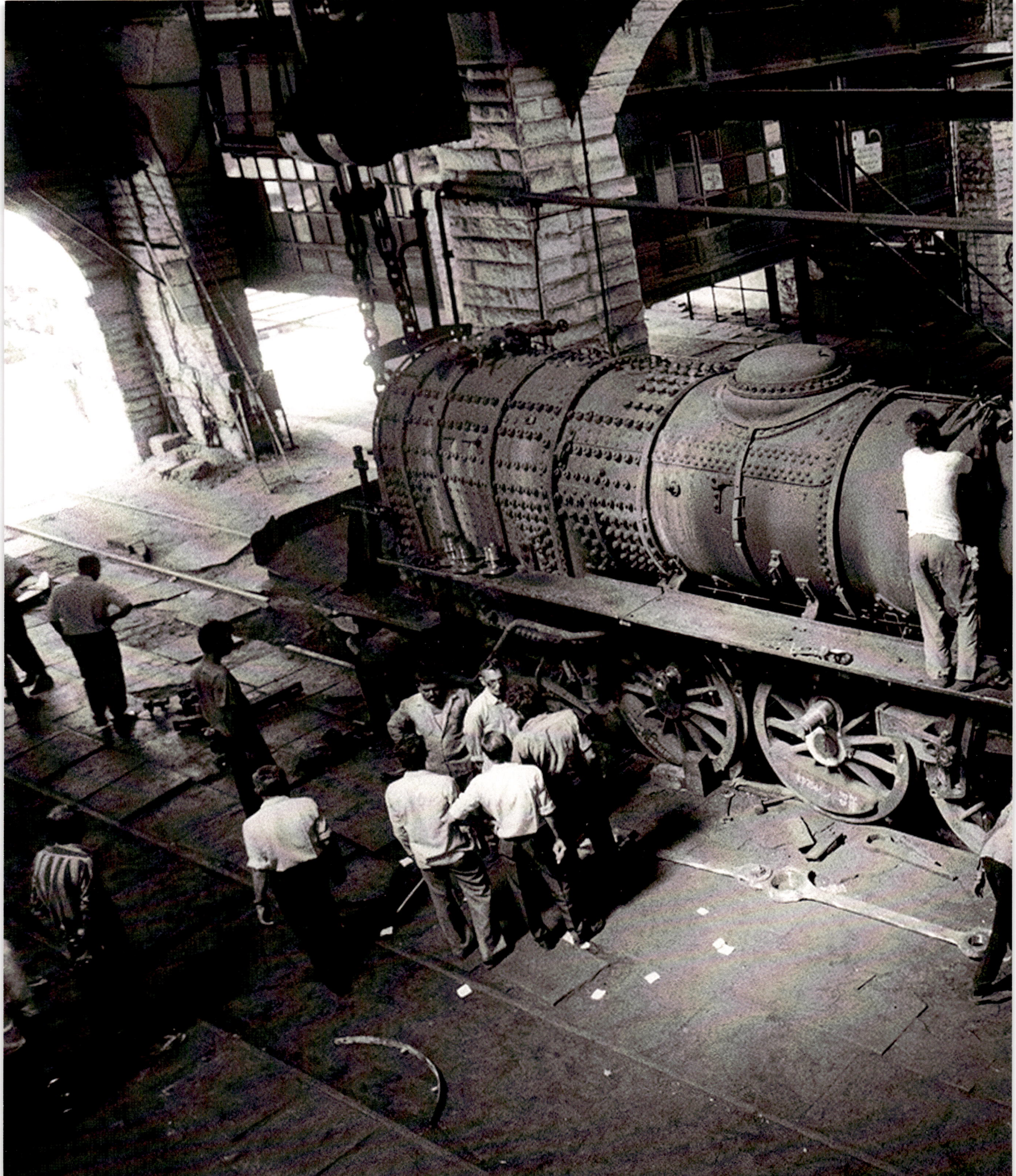

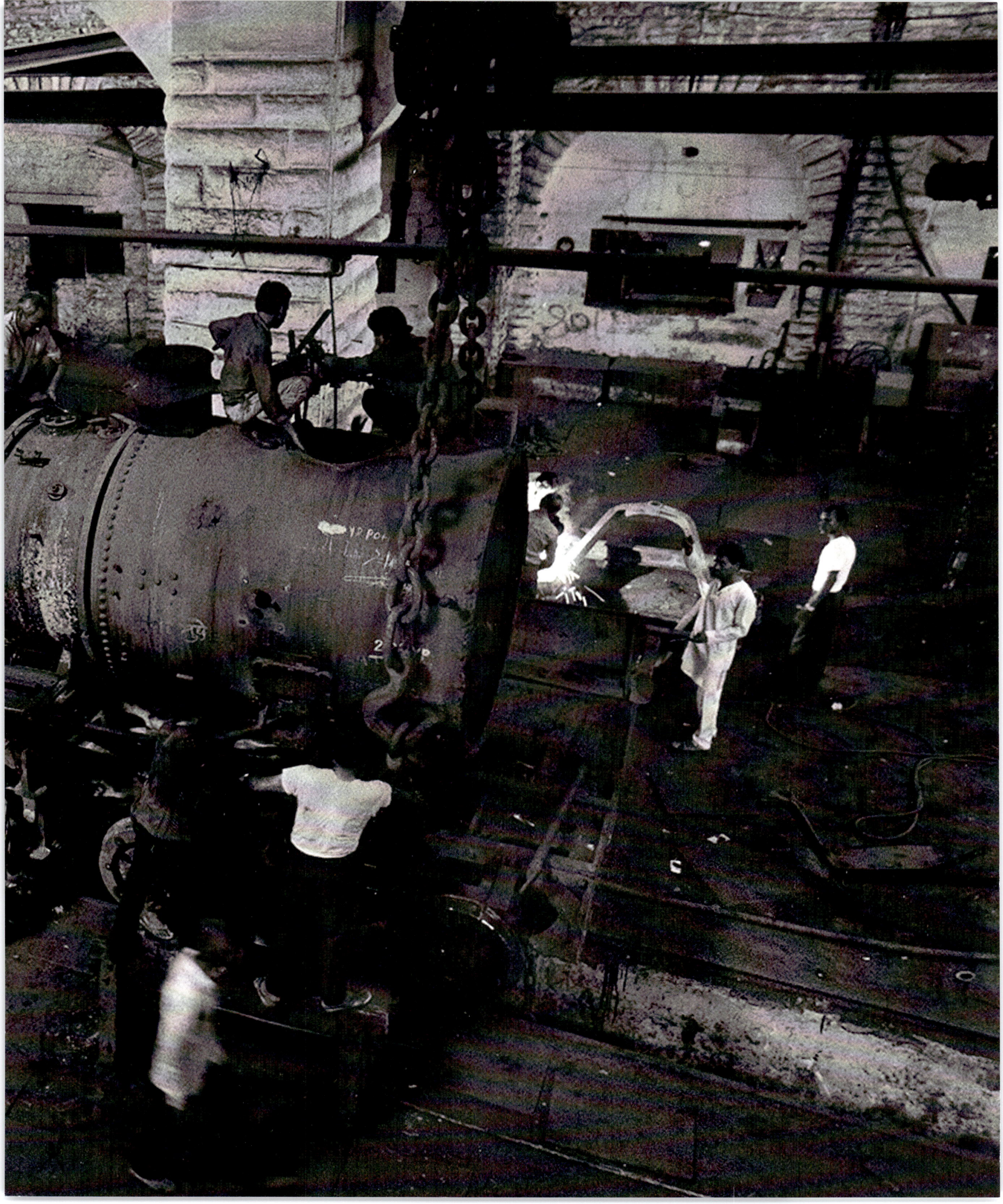

previous page
Erecting shed,
Ajmer locomotive
workshop, Rajastan.

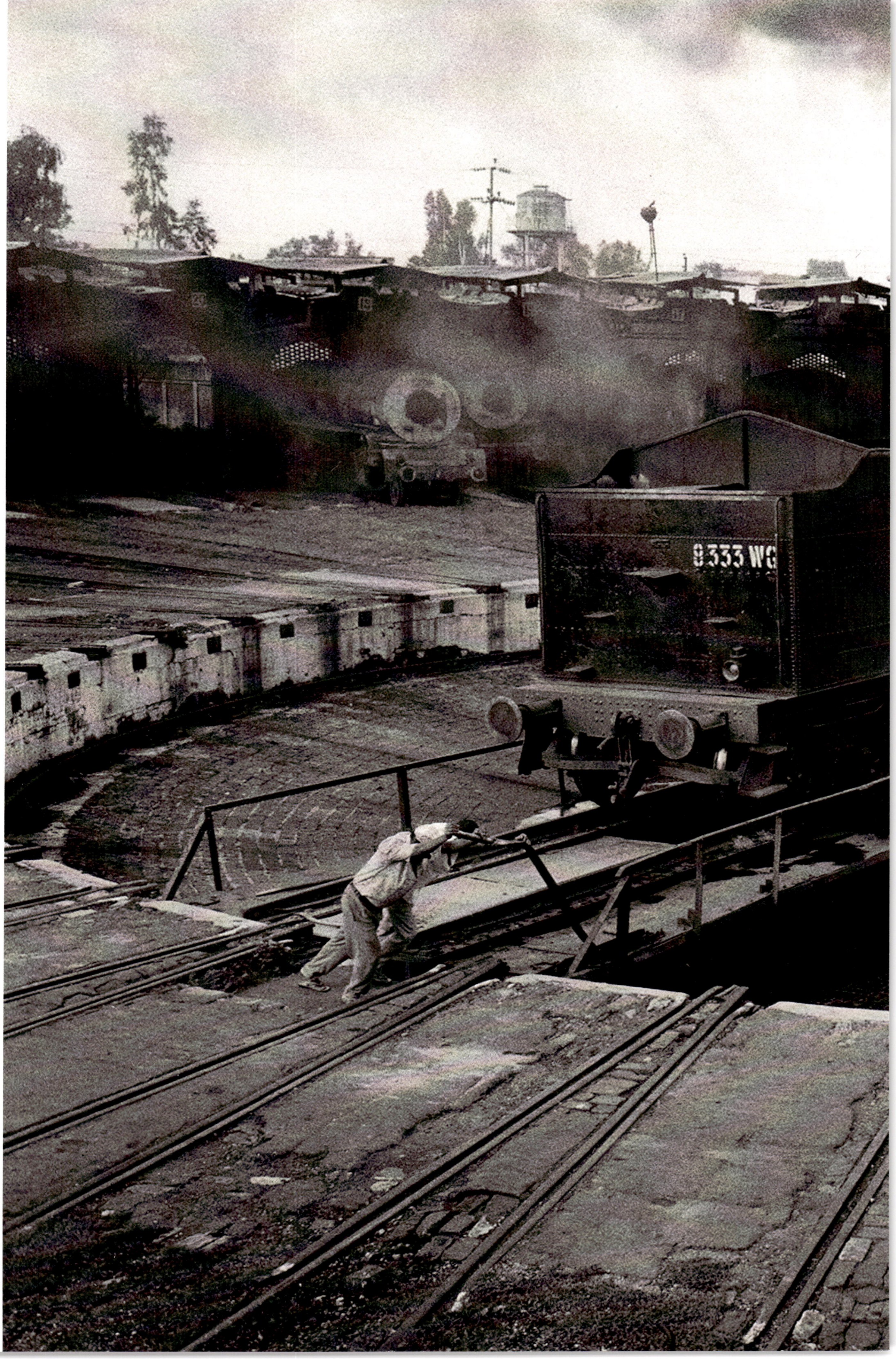

Morabad steam
locomotive shed,
Uttar Pradesh.

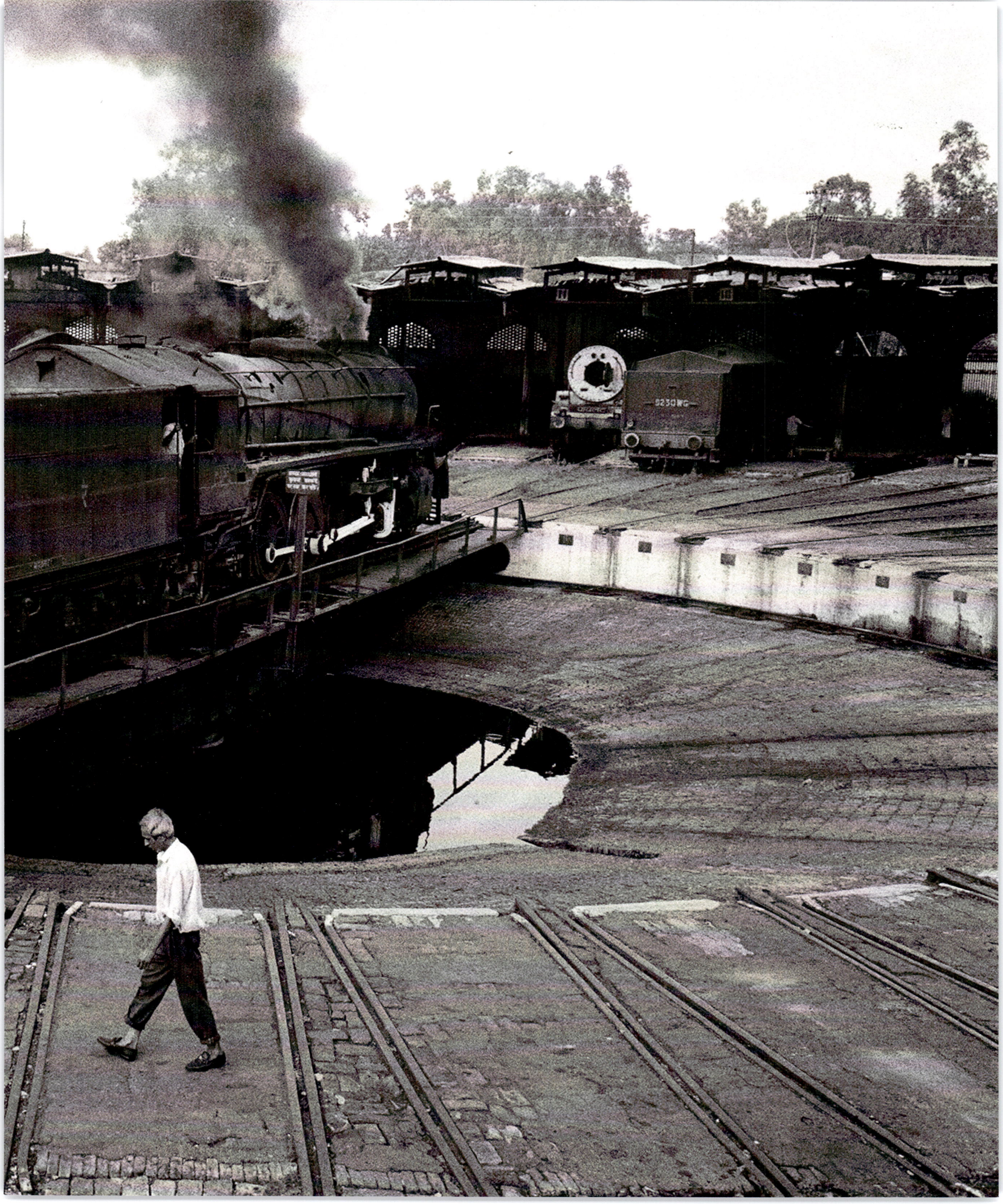
9230 WG

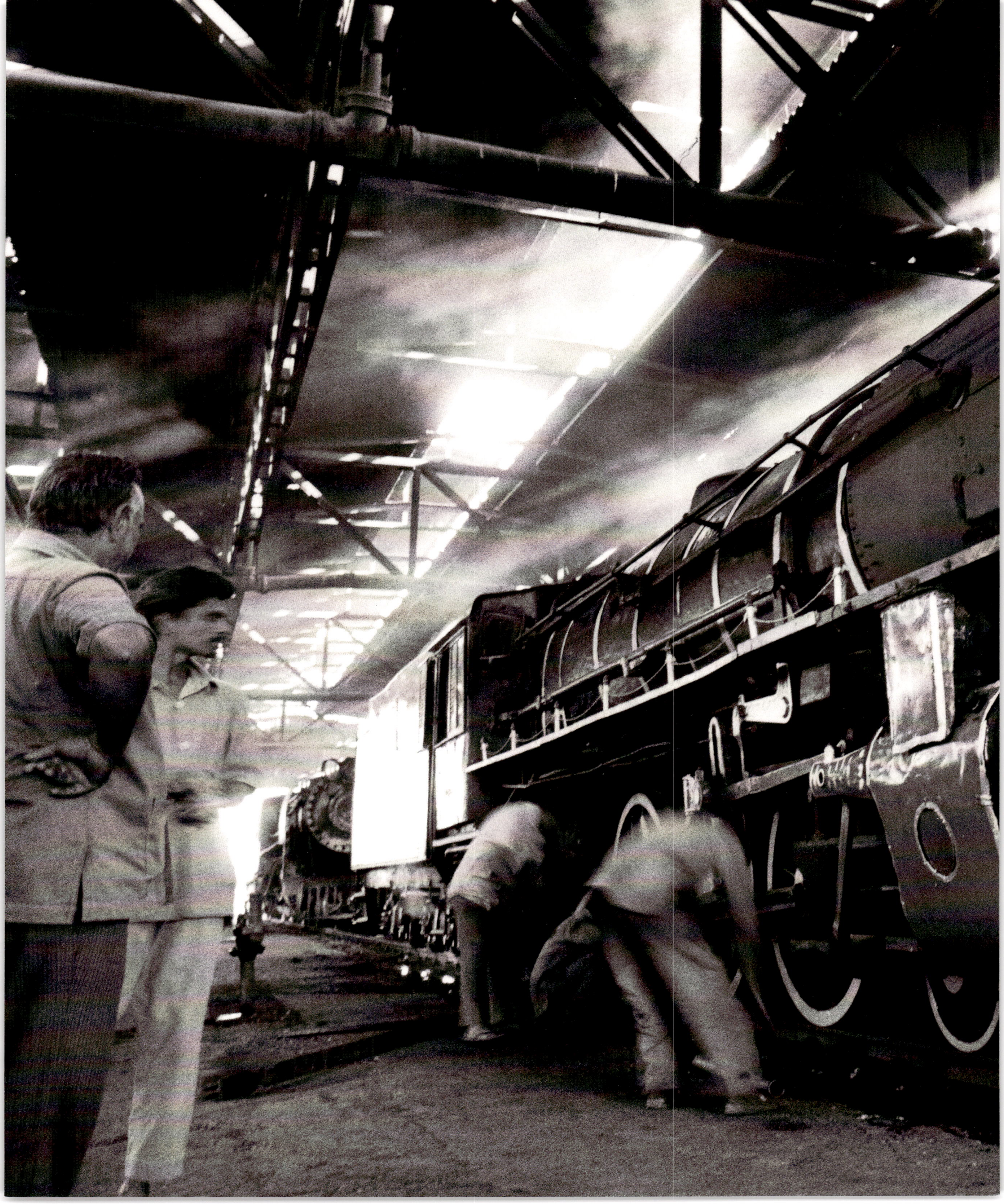

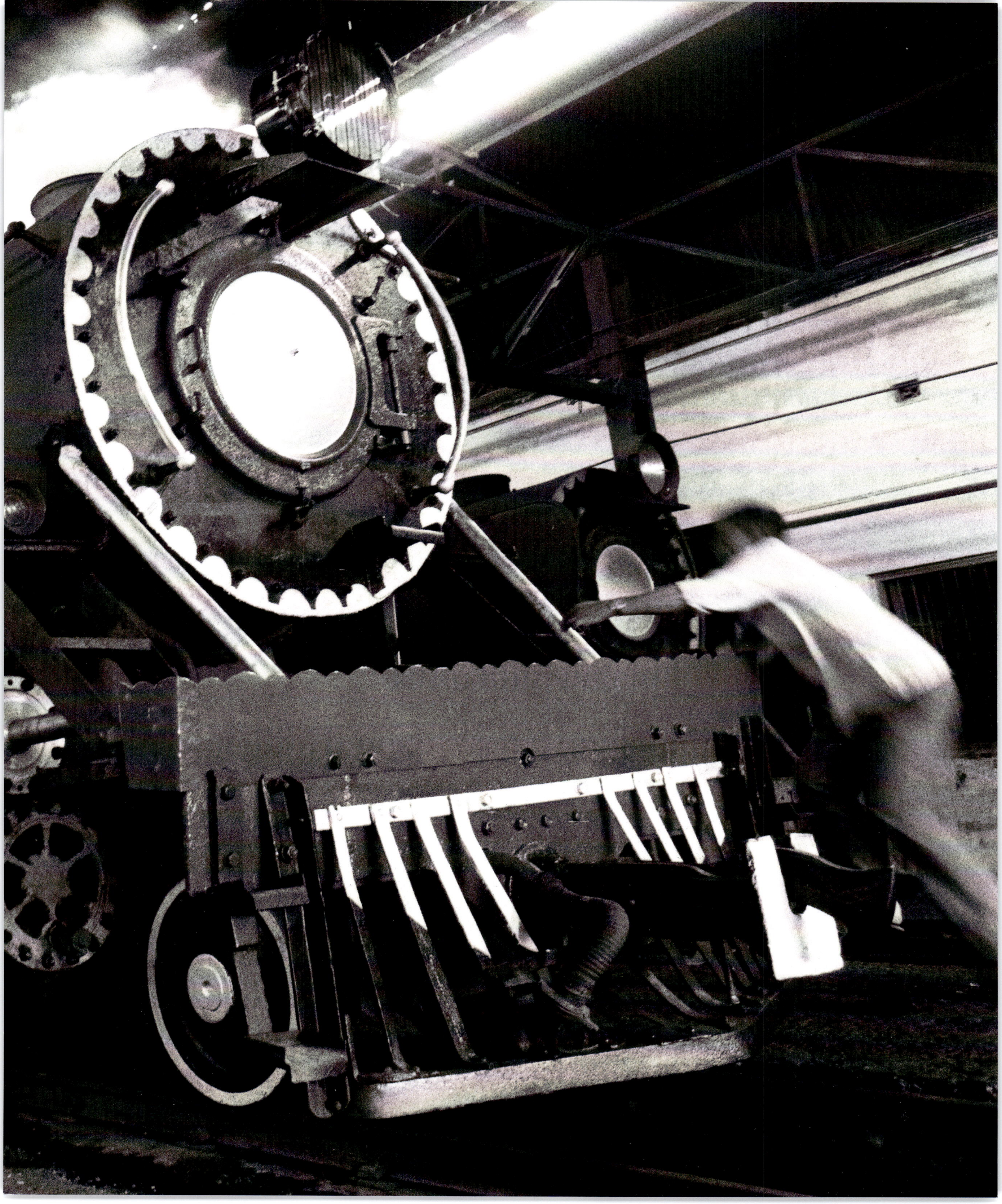

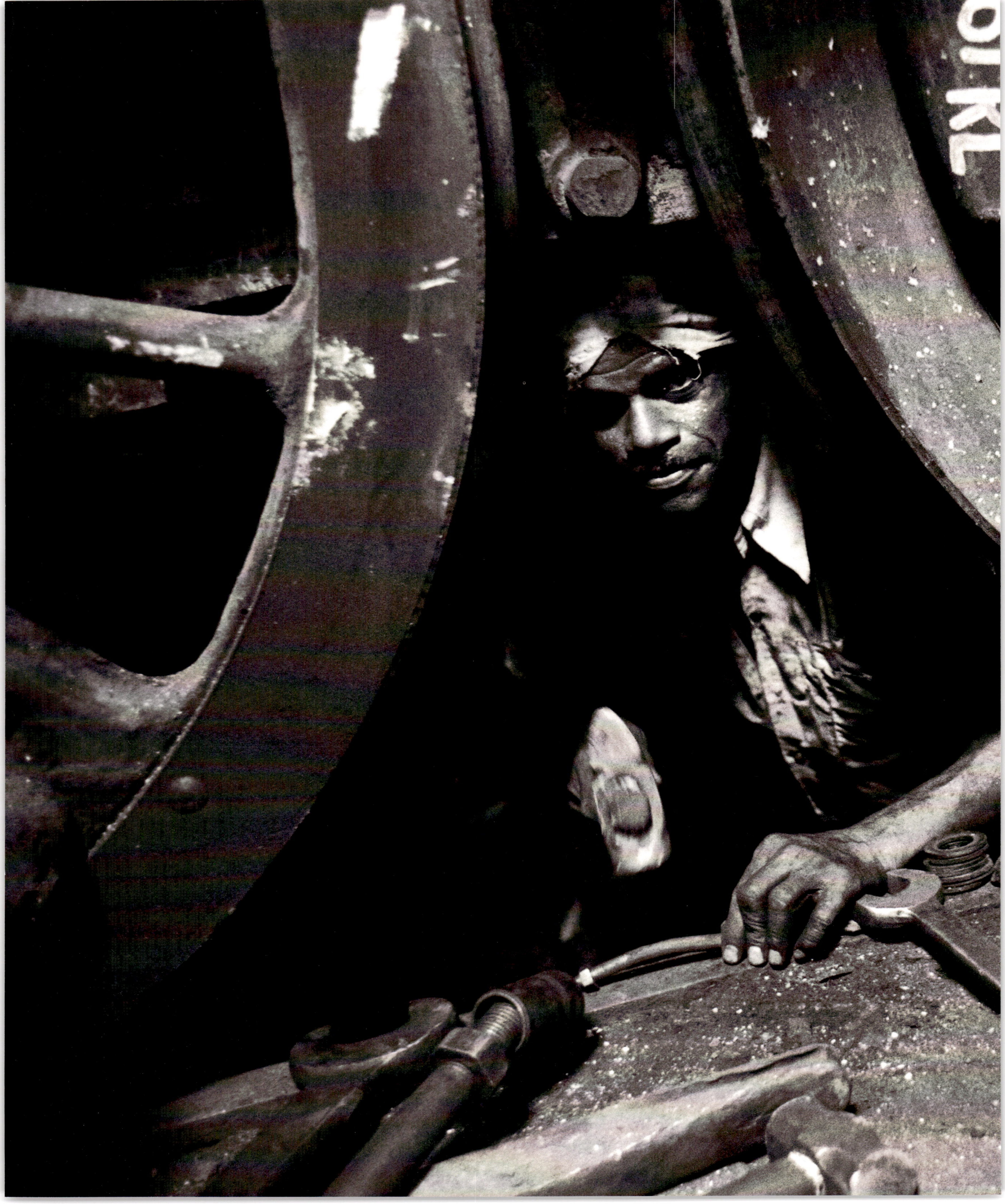

previous page
The last journey
for this engine
and the last day
of work for the
crew of Bareilly
shed before it
closes down,
Uttar Pradesh.

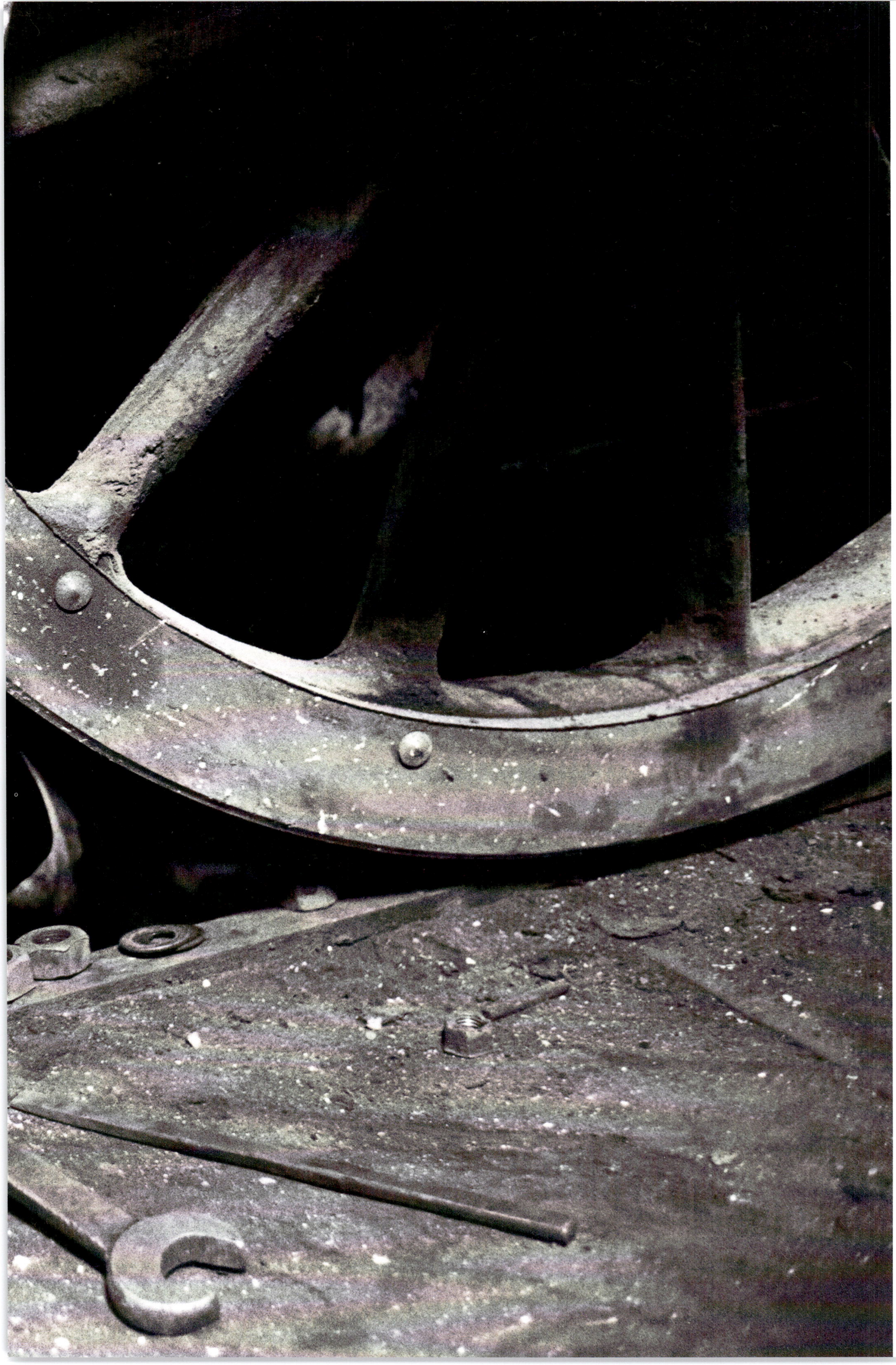

Loco mechanic
Ajmer loco workshop,
Rajastan.

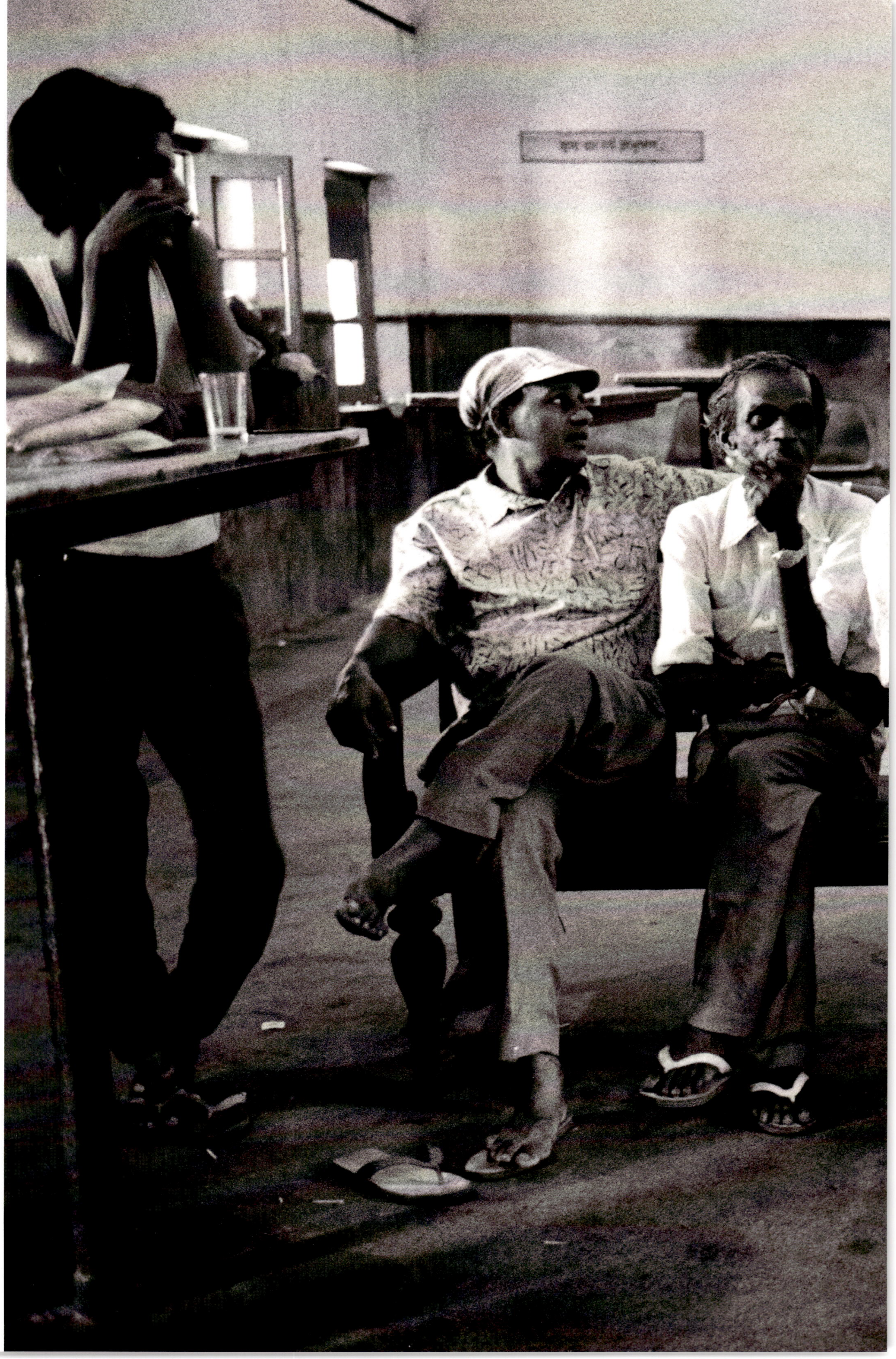

Tea break at
the Moradabad
locomotive shed,
Uttar Pradesh.

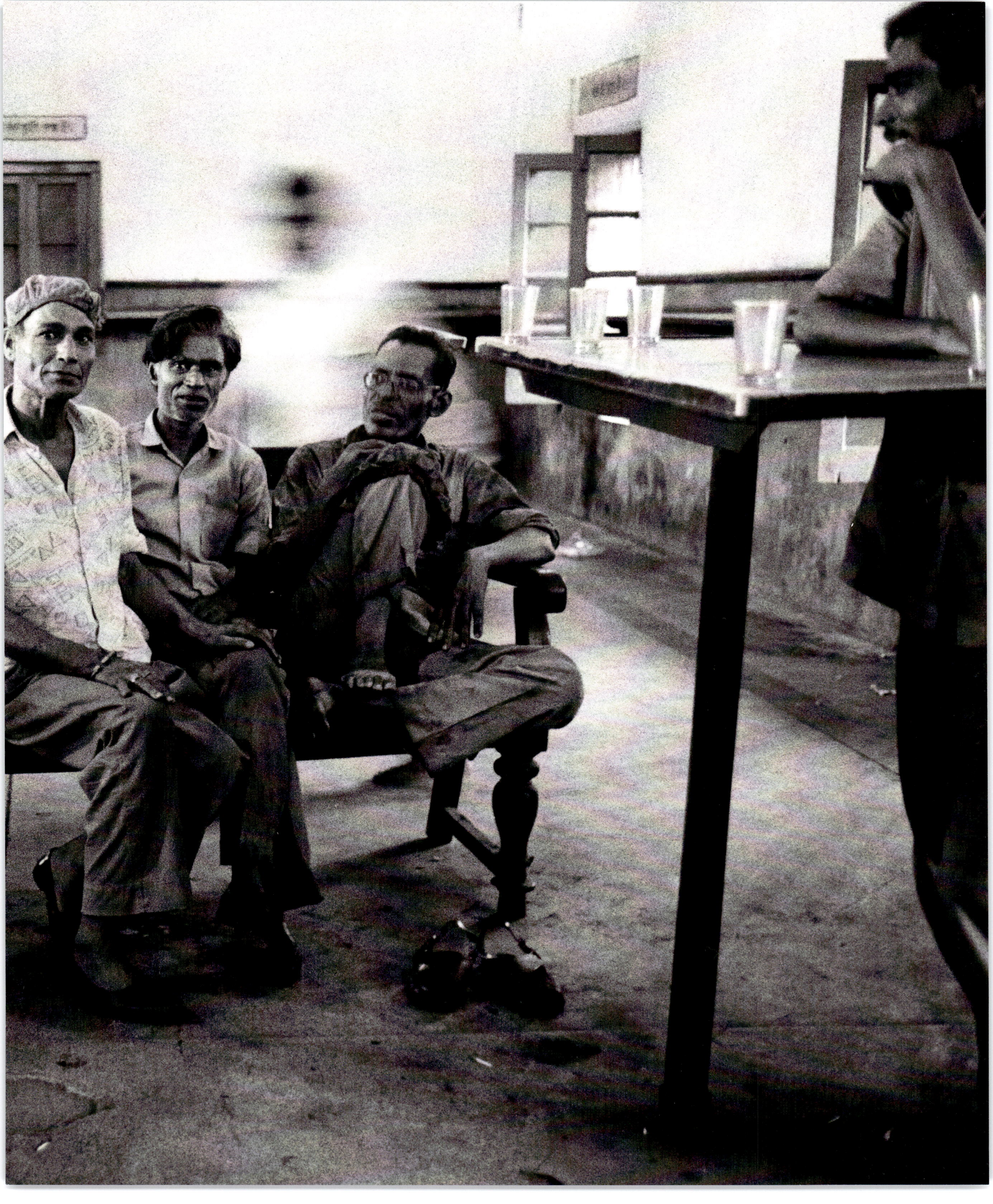

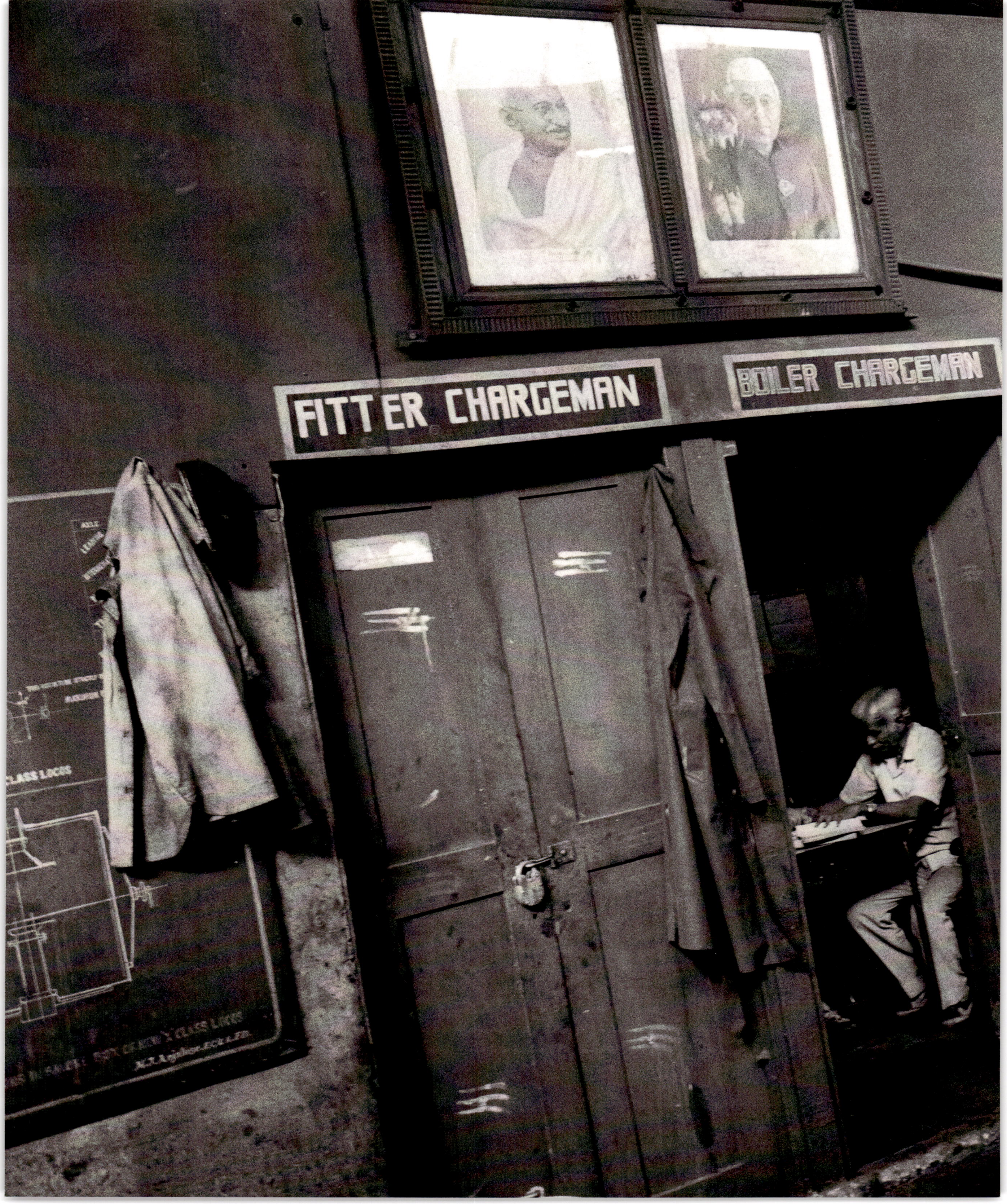
FITTER CHARGEMAN
BOILER CHARGEMAN

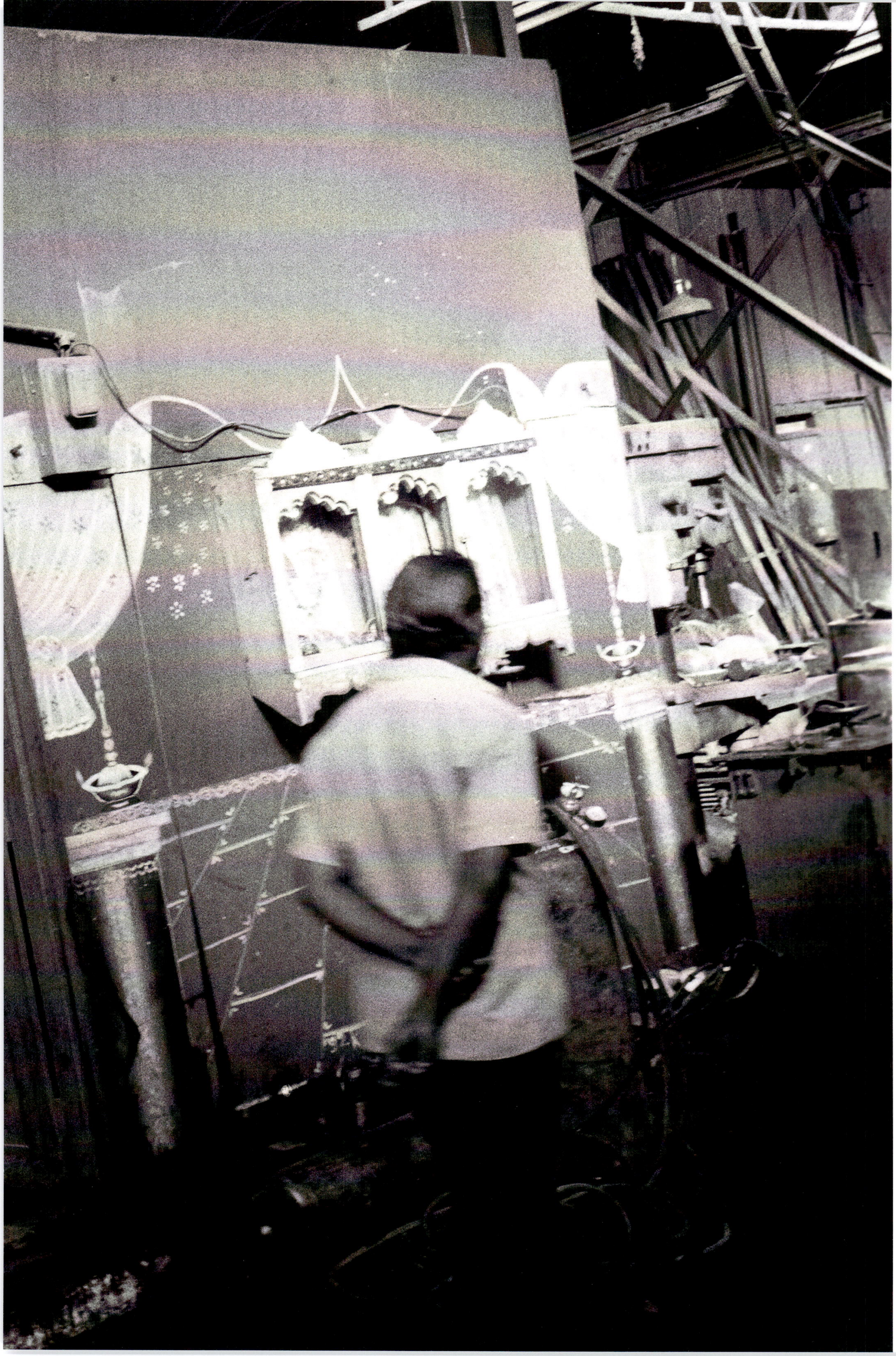

The locomotive
workshop at
Coonoor,
Nilgiri Hills.

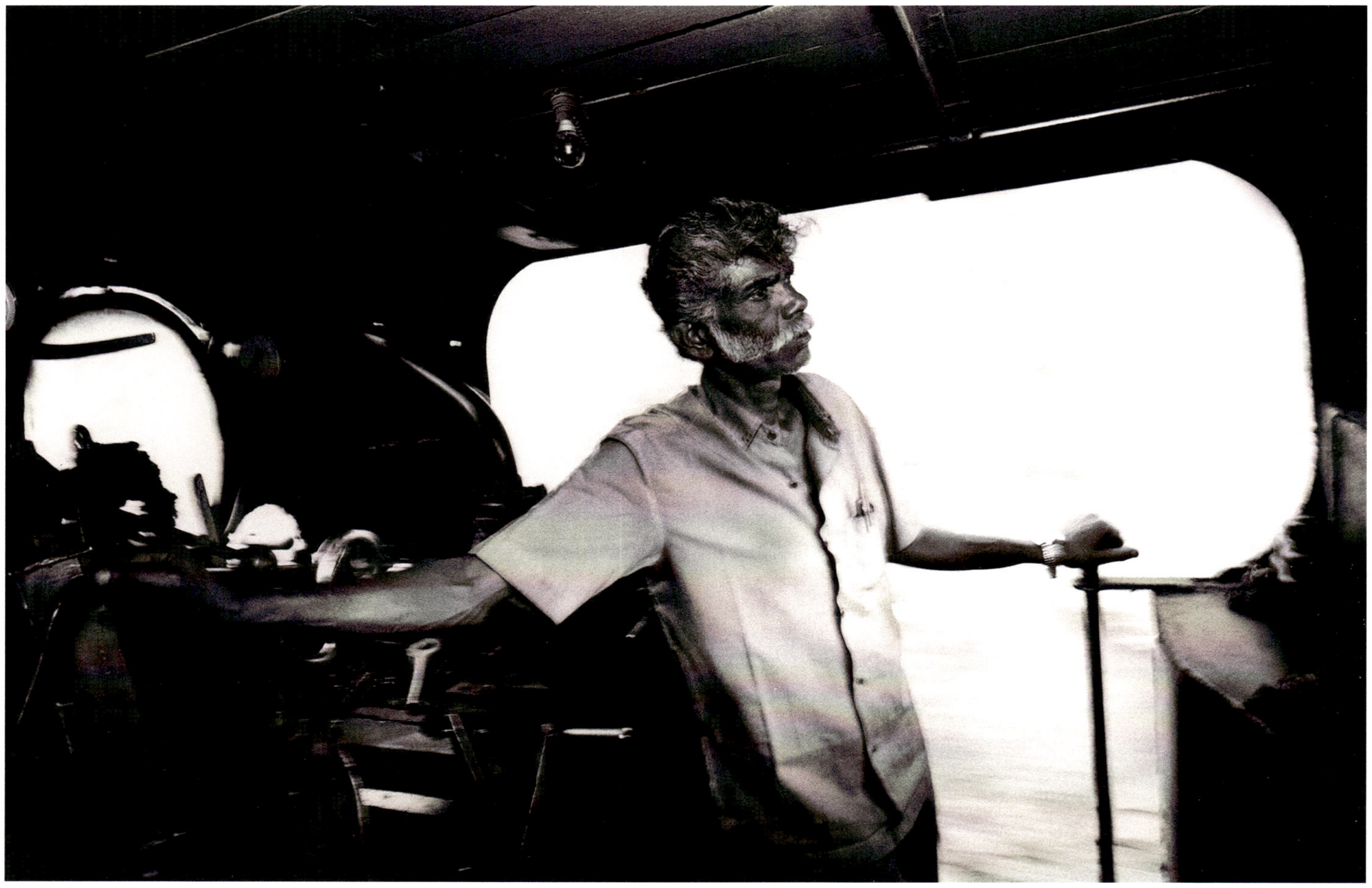

above
Steam loco driver, 'Kuppaswamy', on the Nilgiri Express, Tamil Nadu.

opposite page
A boiler mechanic at Mhow loco shed, Madhya Pradesh.

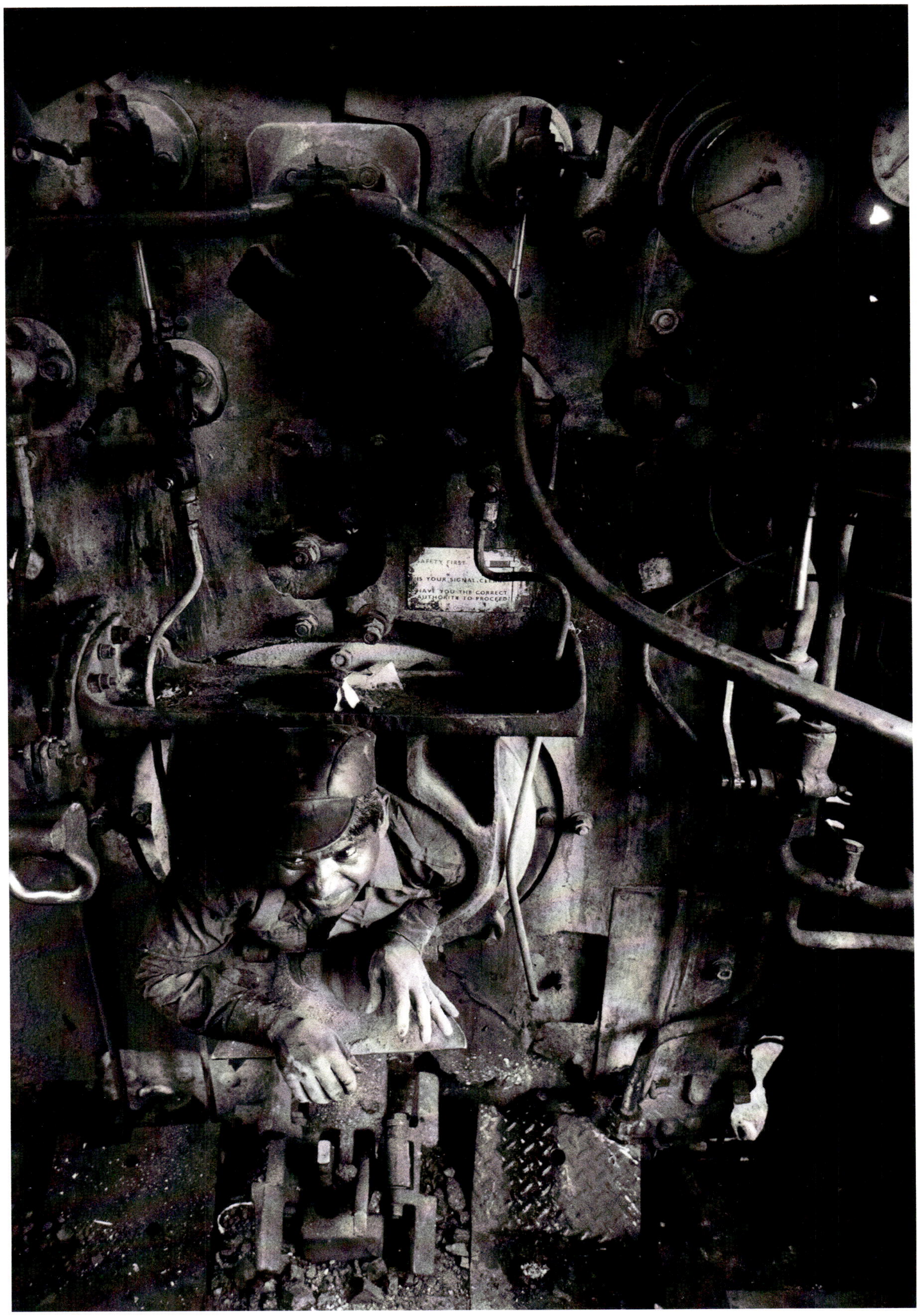
SAFETY FIRST
IS YOUR SIGNAL CL
HAVE YOU THE CORRECT
AUTHORITY TO PROCEED

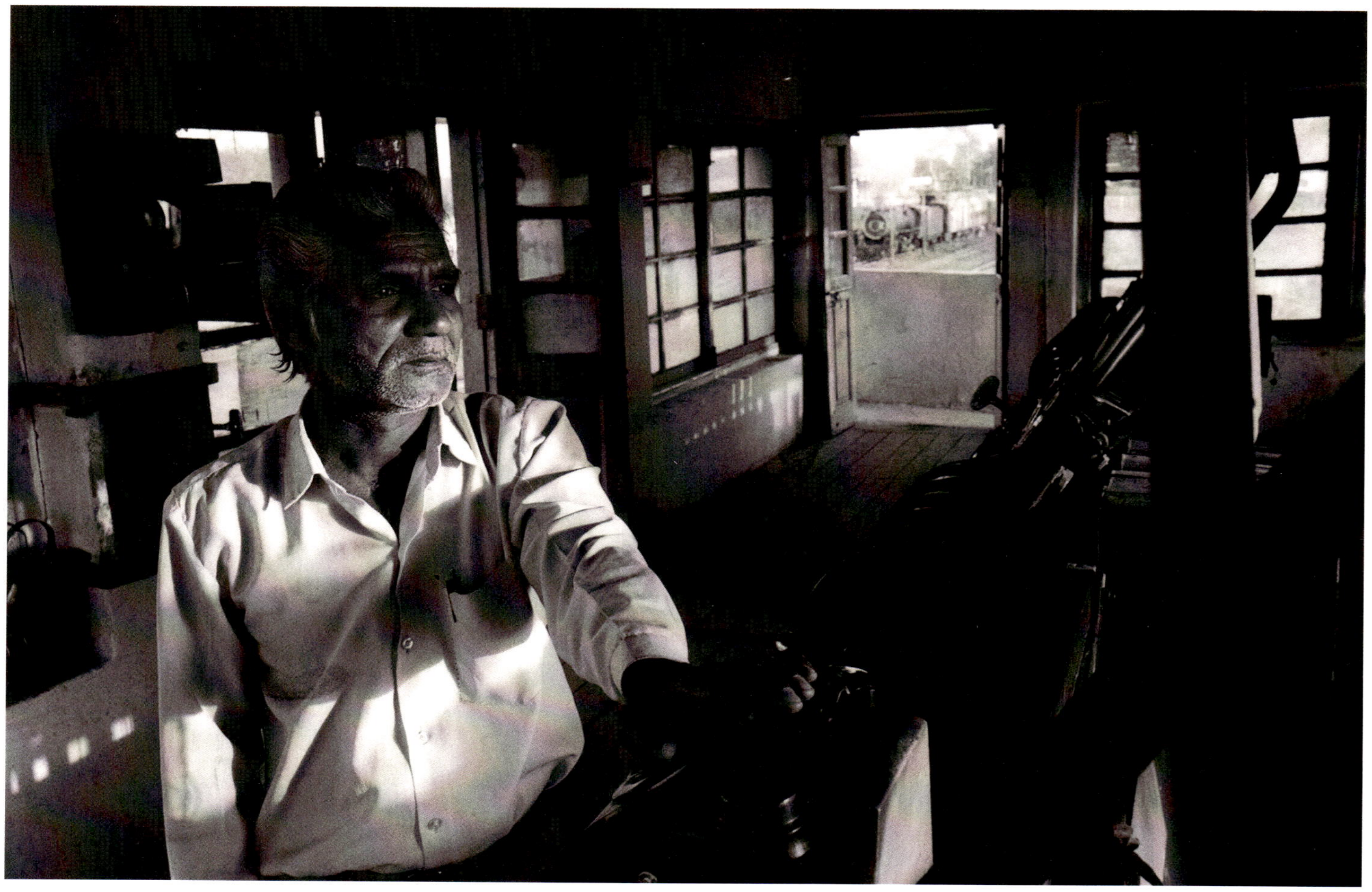

above
A signalman at Mhow railway station, Madhya Pradesh.

opposite page
A signalman walks in front of a steam engine at the base to the Nilgiri Hills, Tamil Nadu.

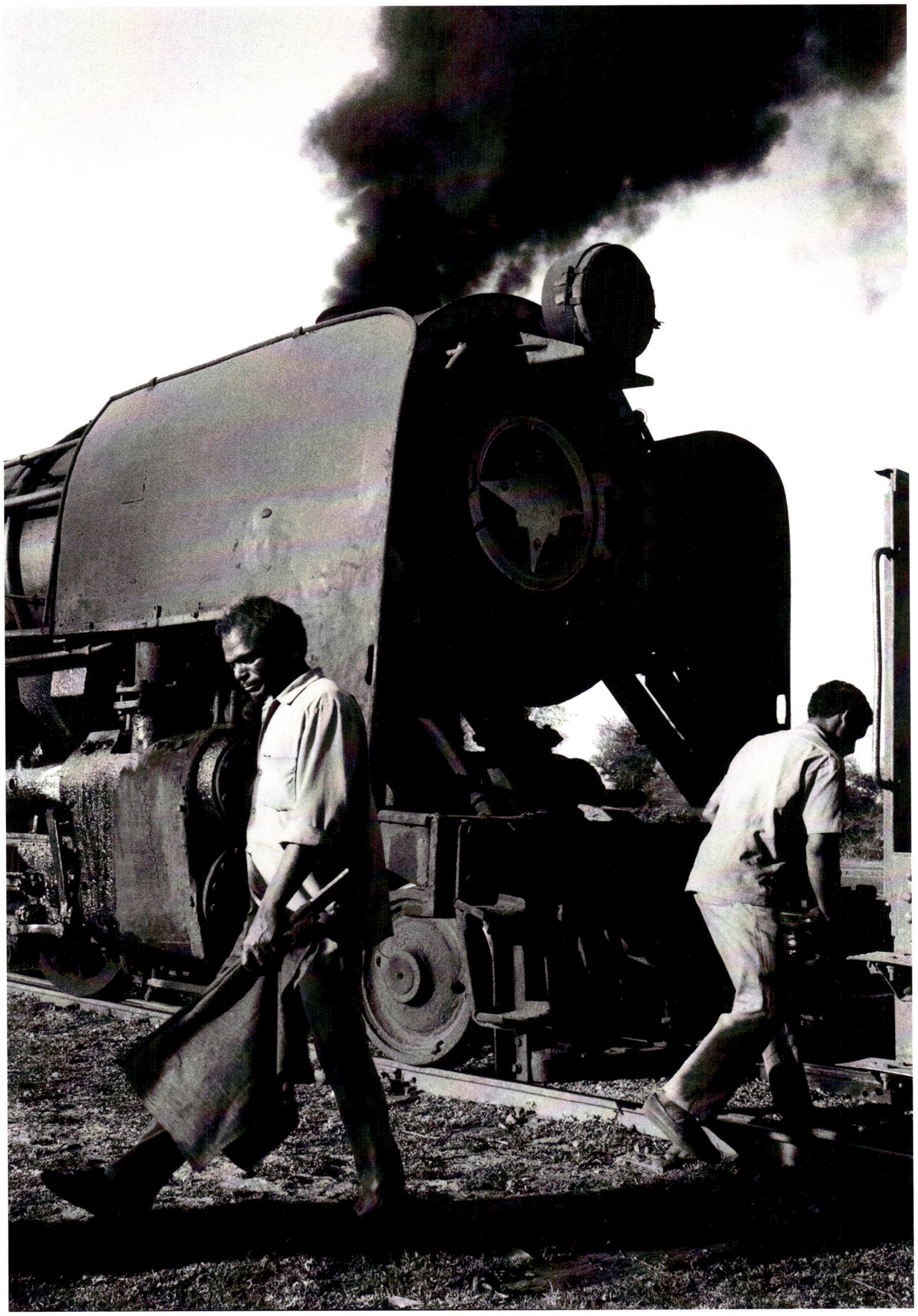

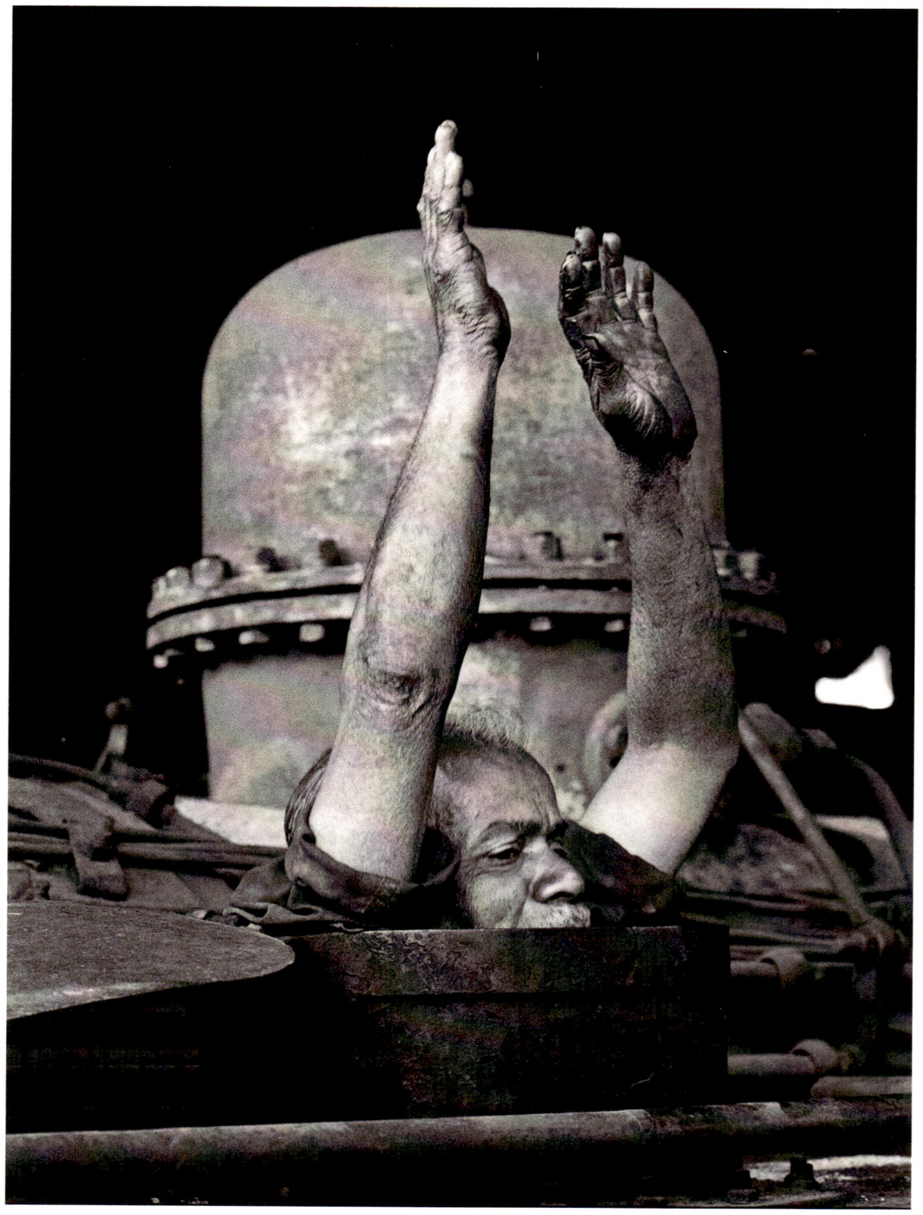

above
Worker squeezes inside a section of a steam engine's boiler,
Coonoor loco shed, Nilgiri Hills, Tamil Nadu.

opposite page
Anglo-Indian worker, Ajmer loco workshop, Rajastan.

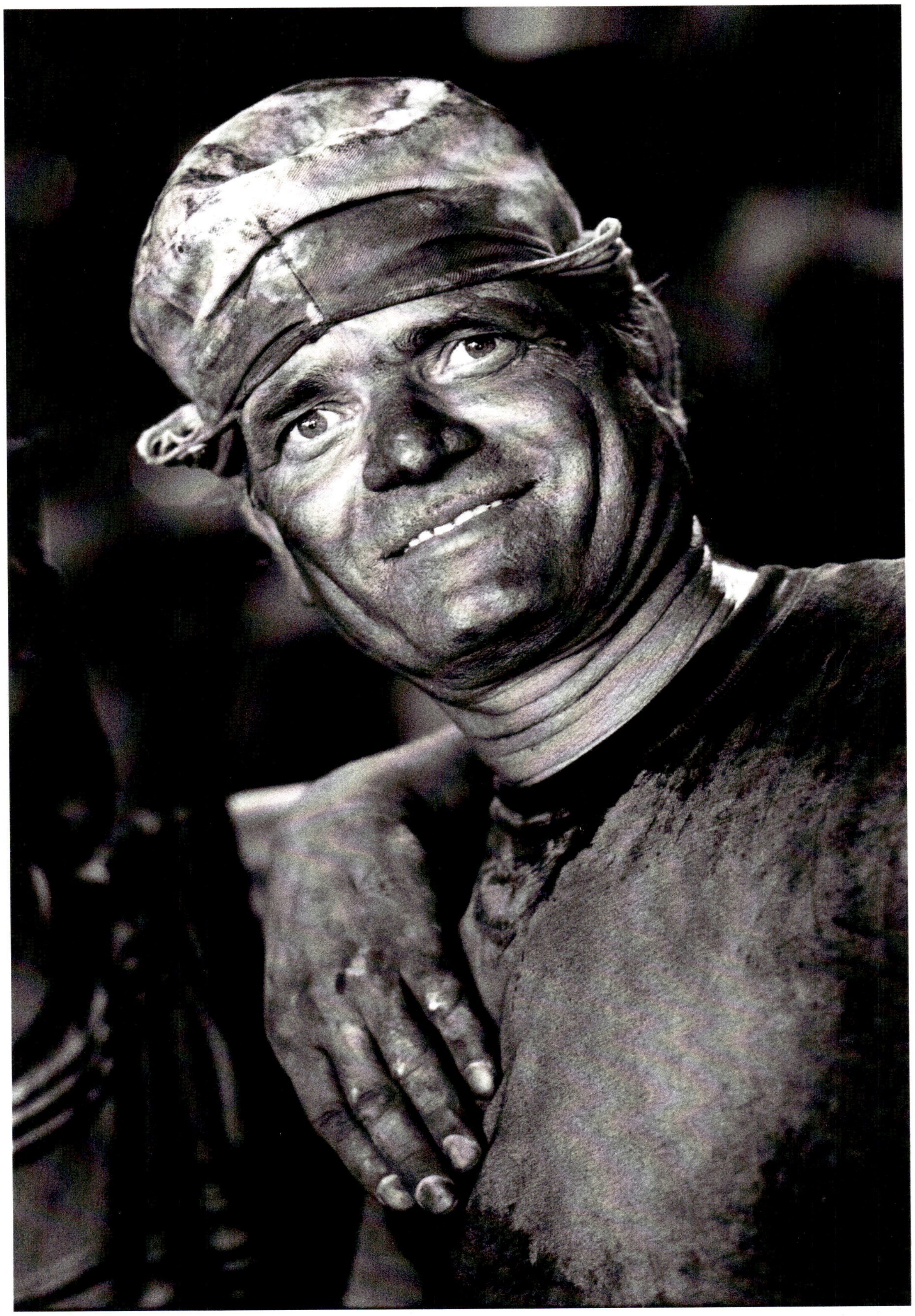

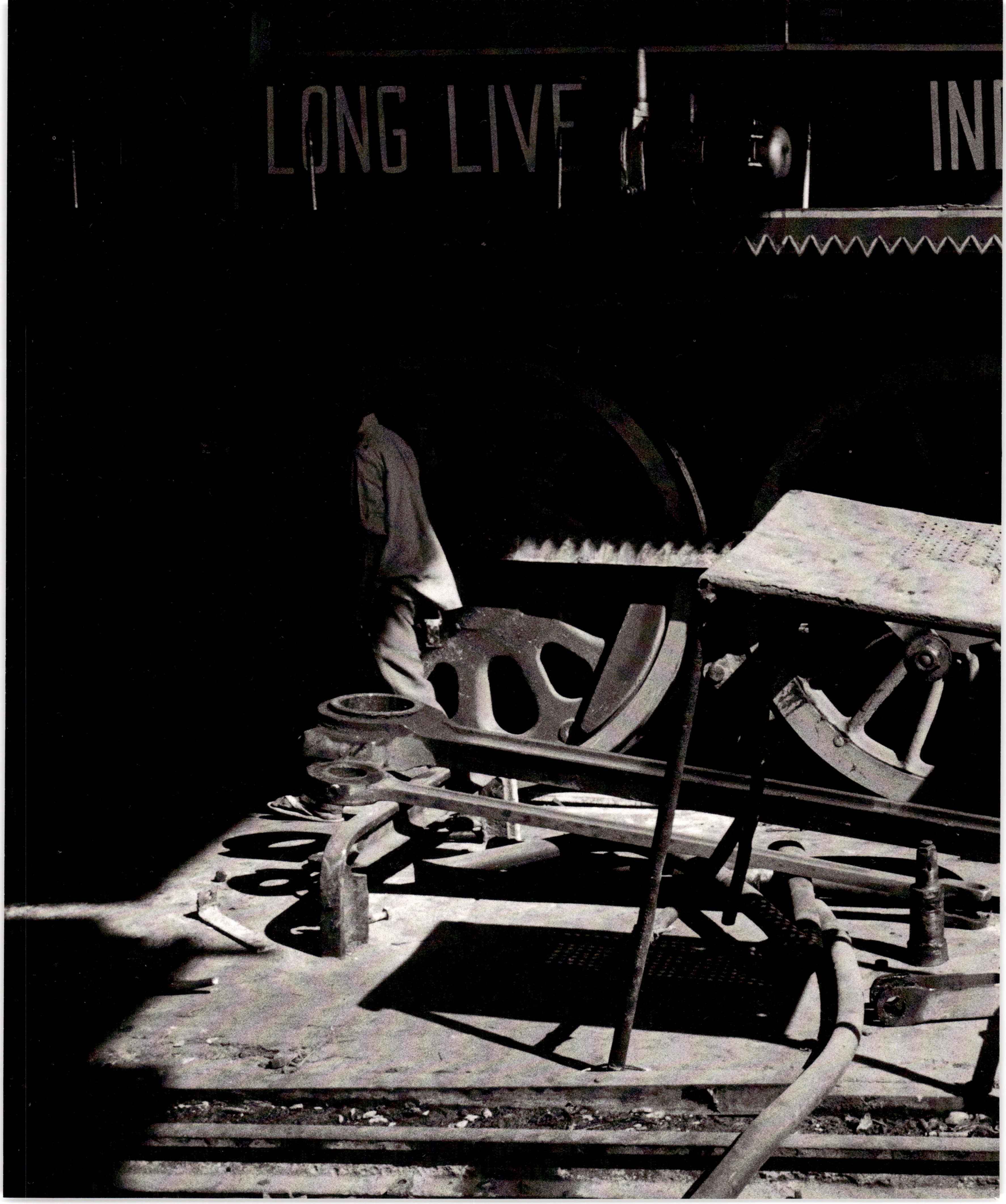
LONG LIVE

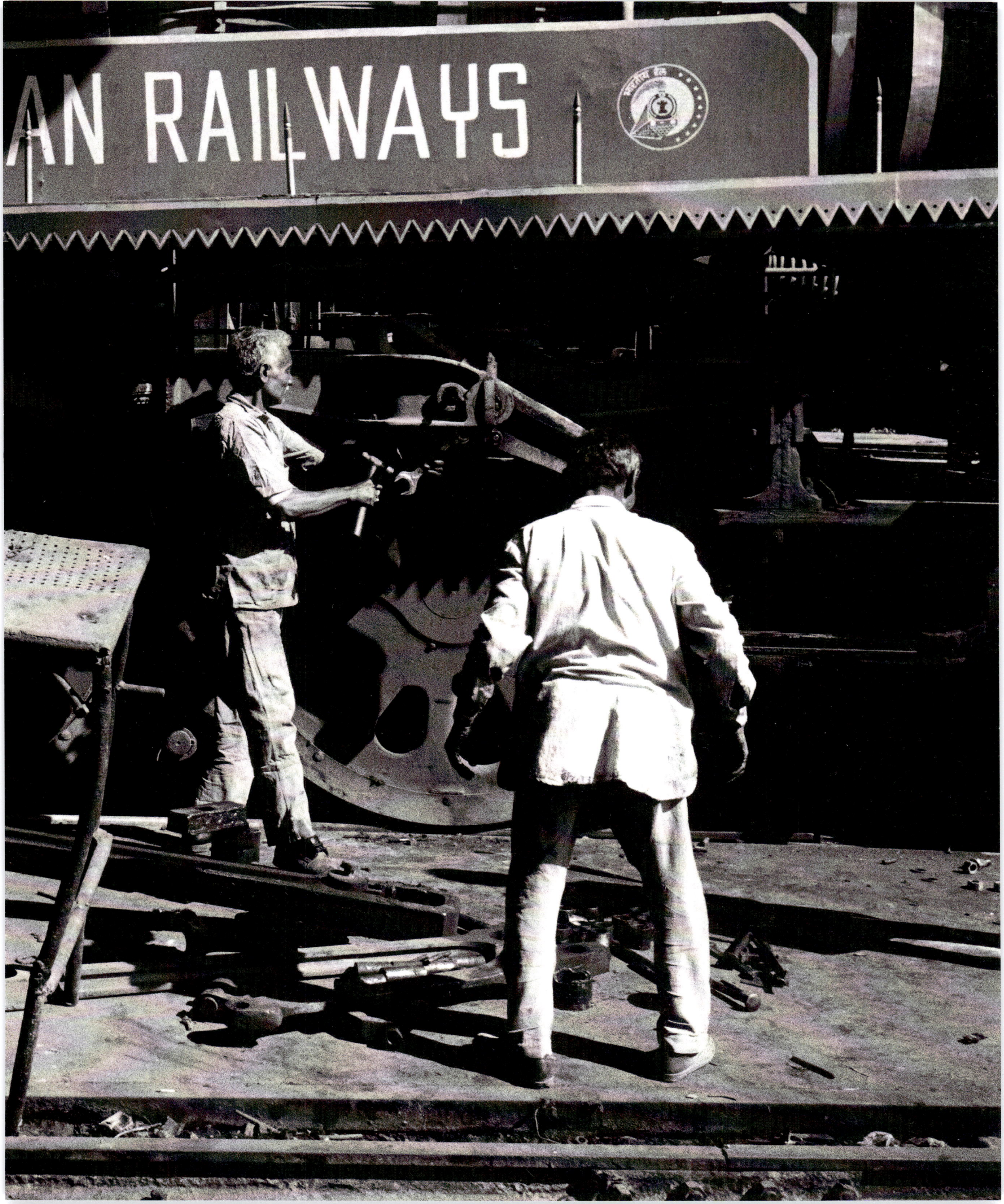
AN RAILWAYS

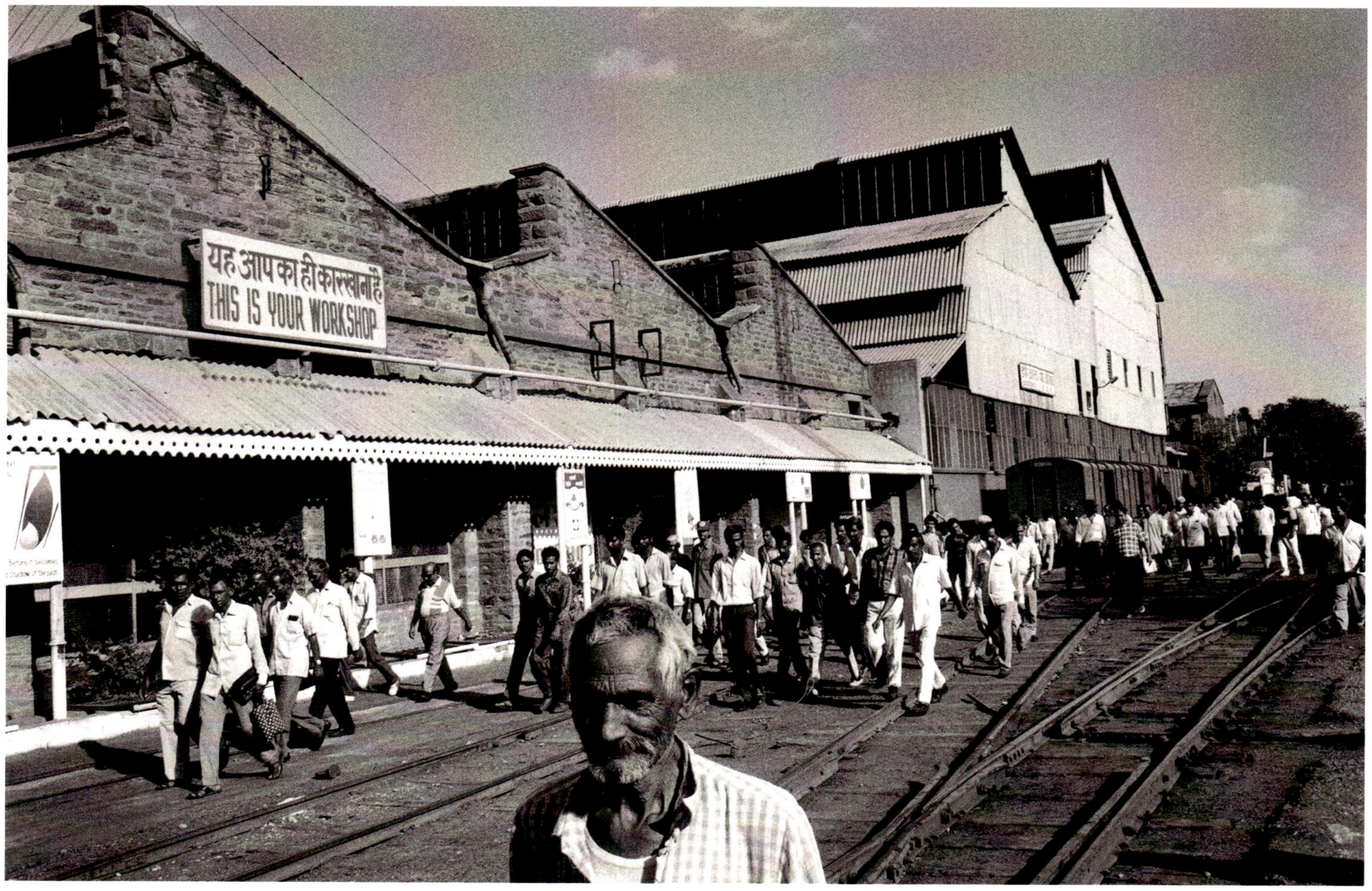

above
The end of the day's work for these men. Ajmer steam loco workshop, Rajastan.

opposite page
Workers at Pratap Nagar loco shed, Rajastan.

previous page
Workers put the final touches on this steam engine in preparation for its last journey. Bareilly steam loco shed, Uttar Pradesh.

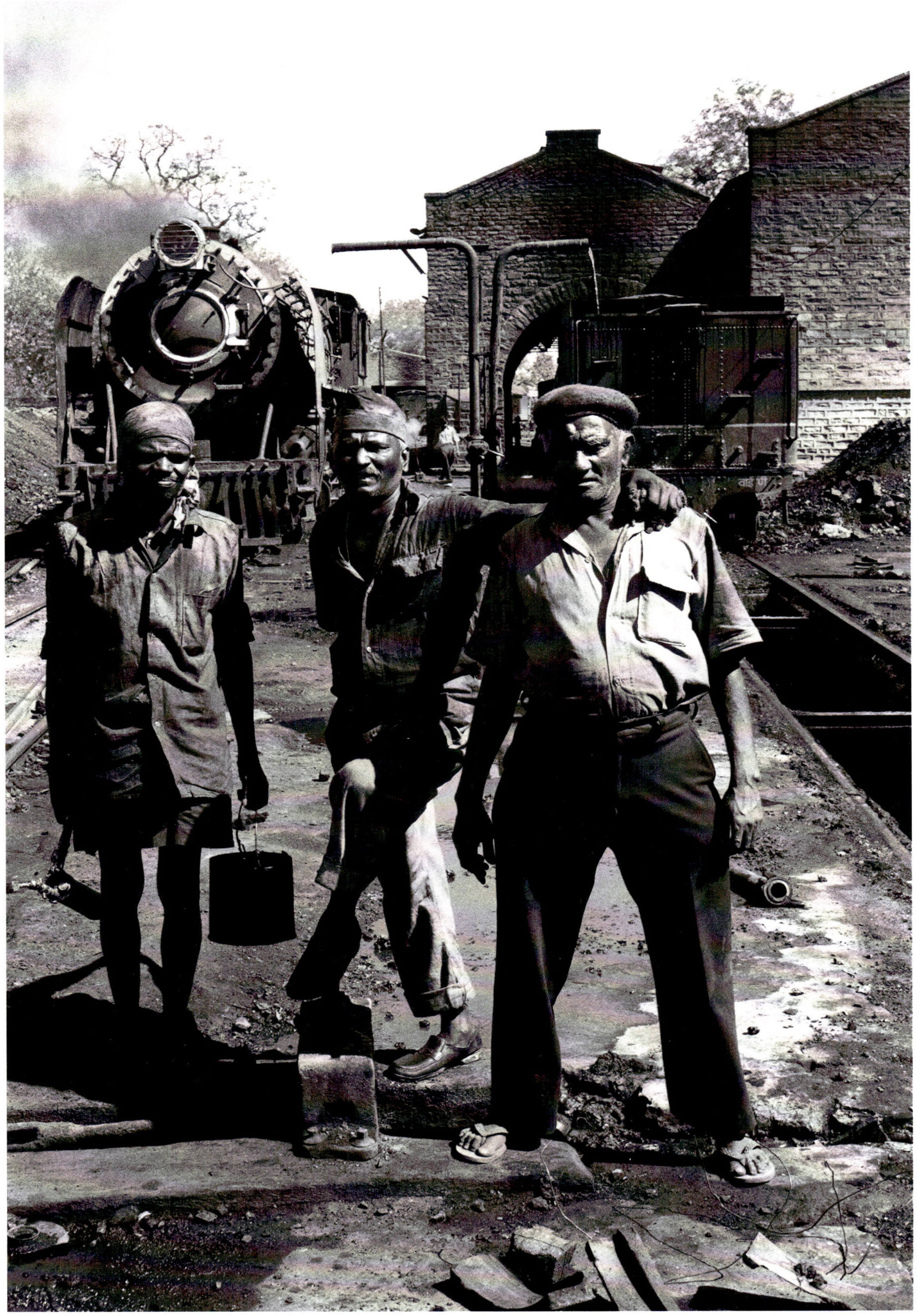

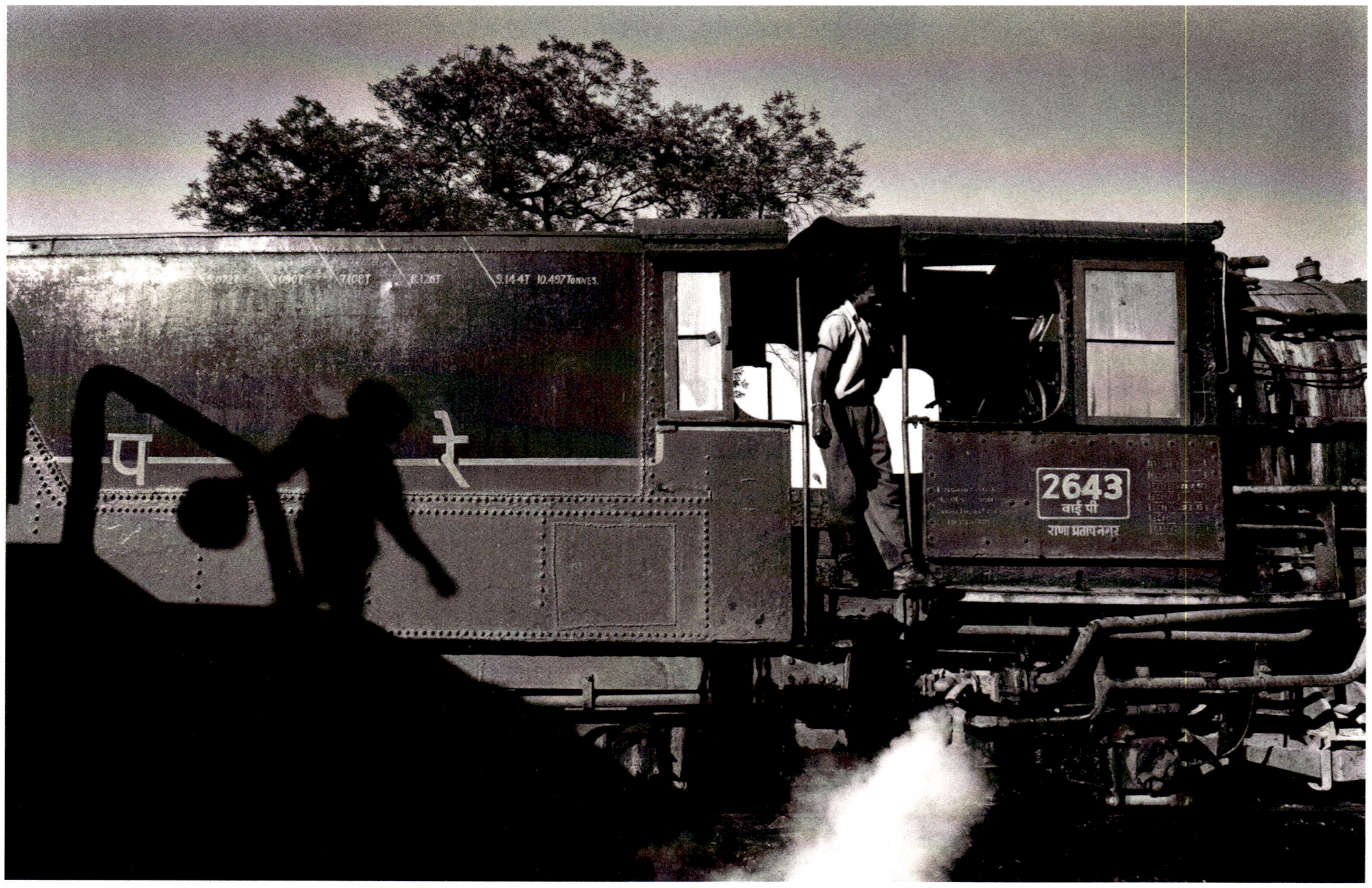

both photographs
Loading the steam engine with water and coal,
Rana Pratap Nagar loco shed, Rajastan.

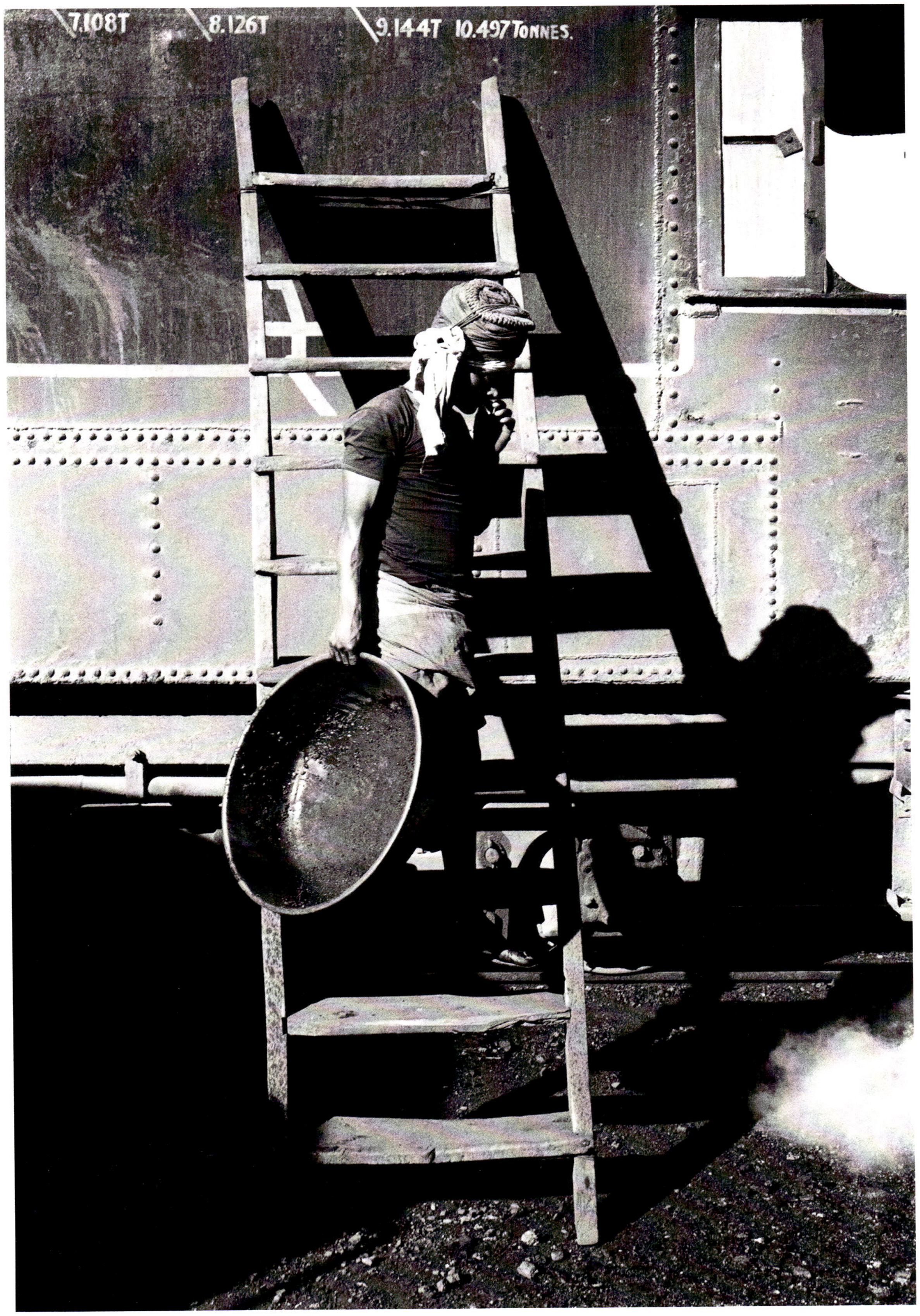
7.108T
8.126T
9.144T 10.497 TONNES.

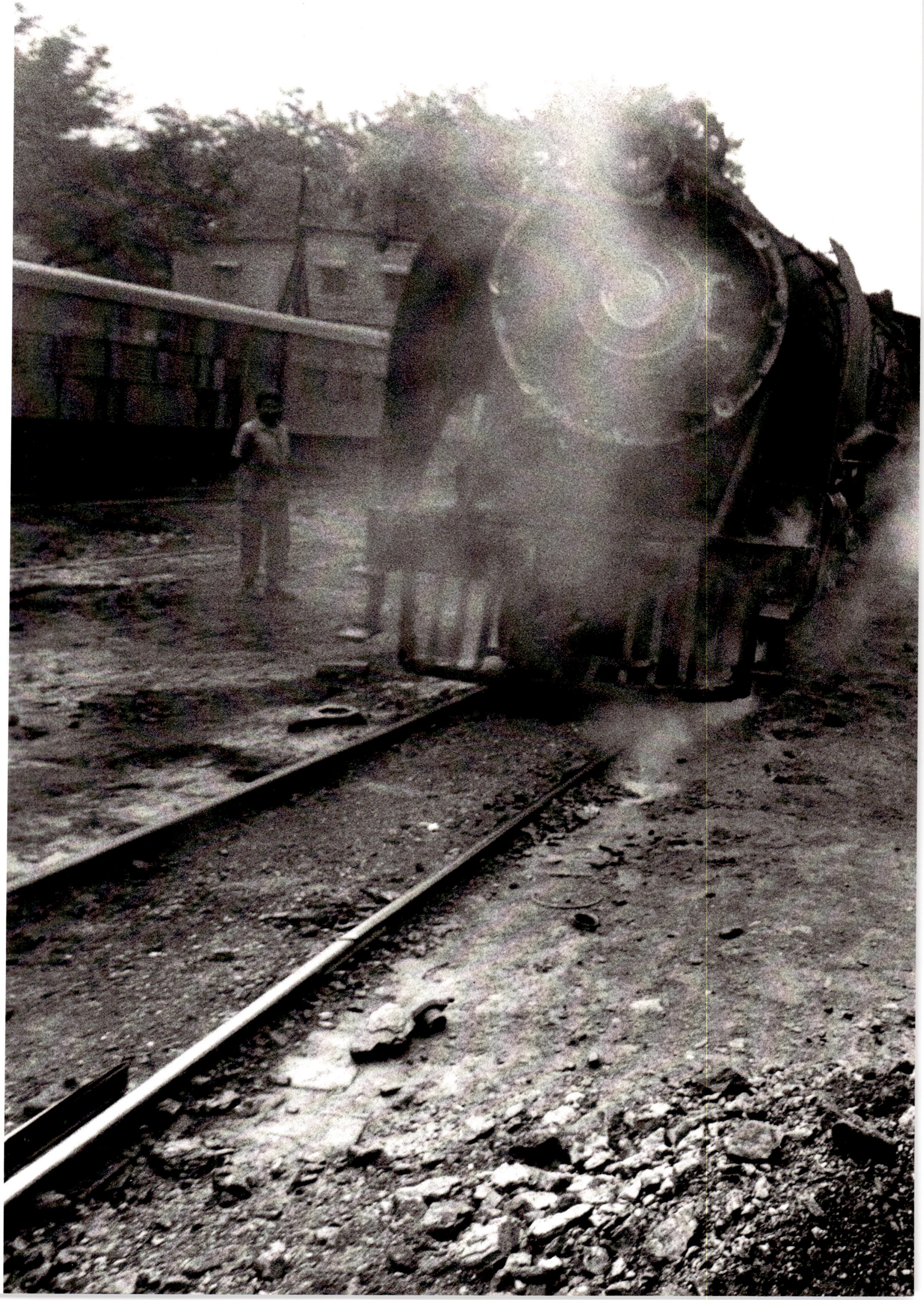

A worker takes
a rest inside
a coal wagon.
Rana Pratap Nagar
loco shed, Rajastan.

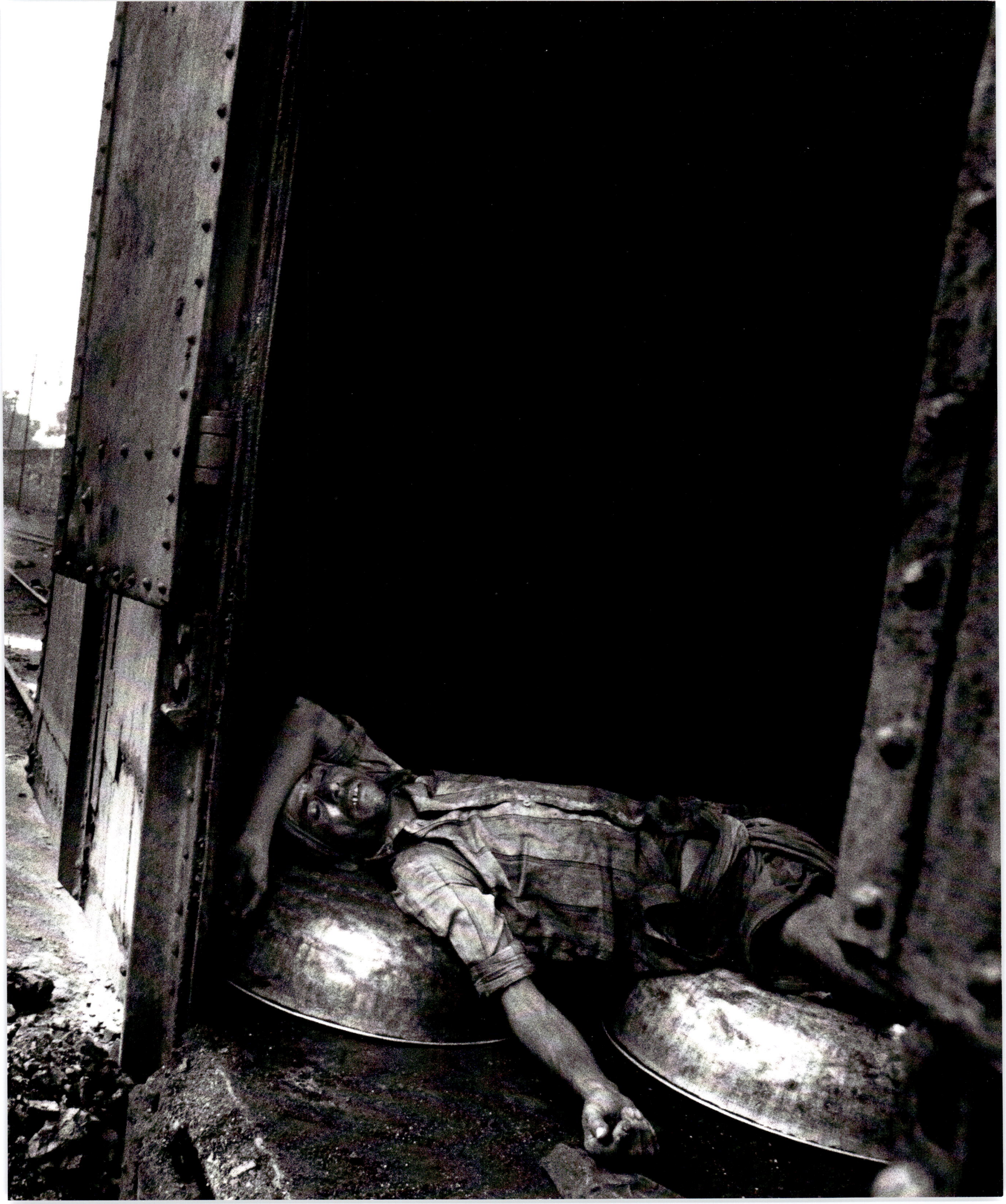

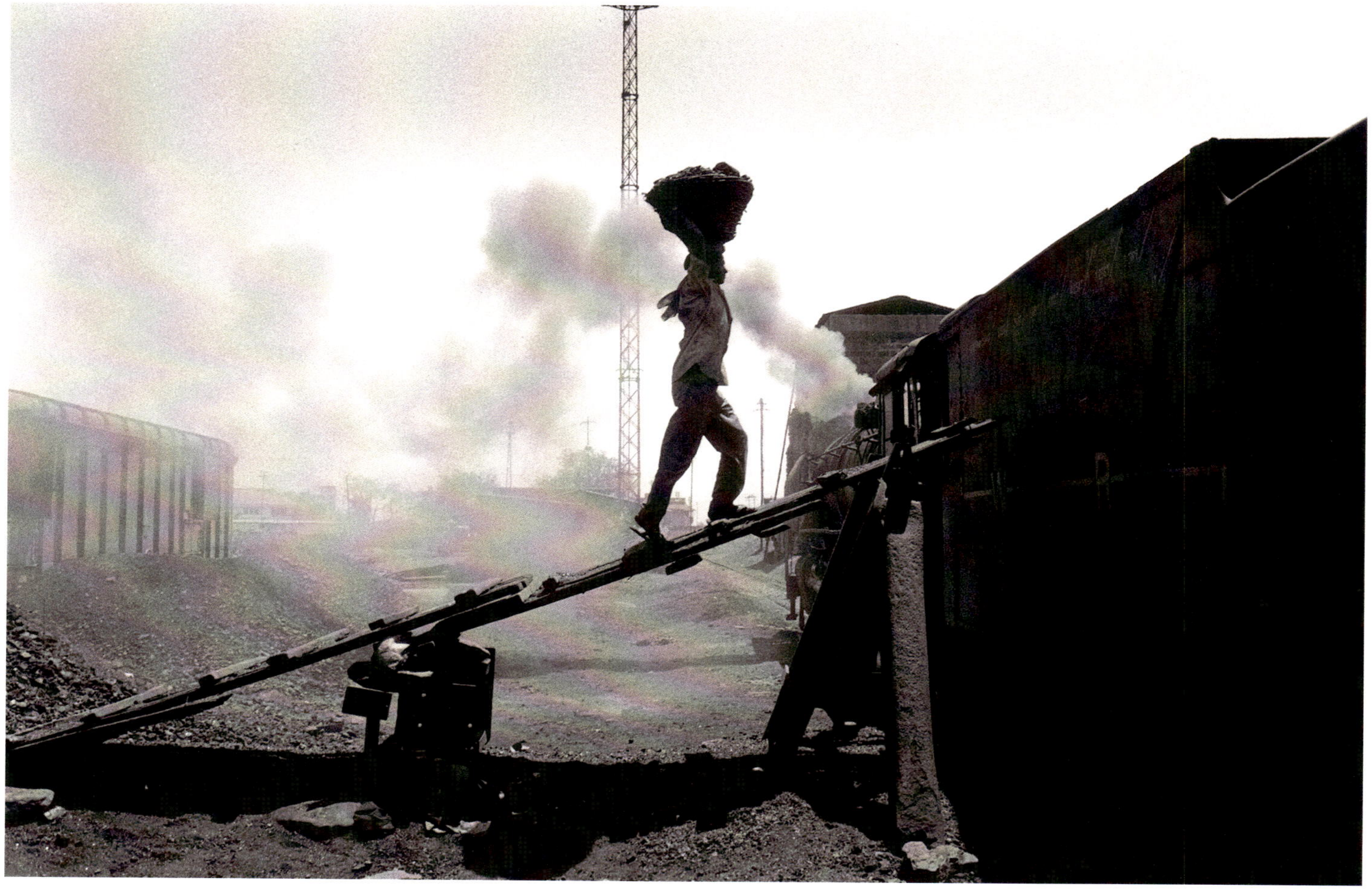

Loading coal.
Ratlam, Madhya Pradesh *(above)*.
Rana Pratap Nagar *(right)*.

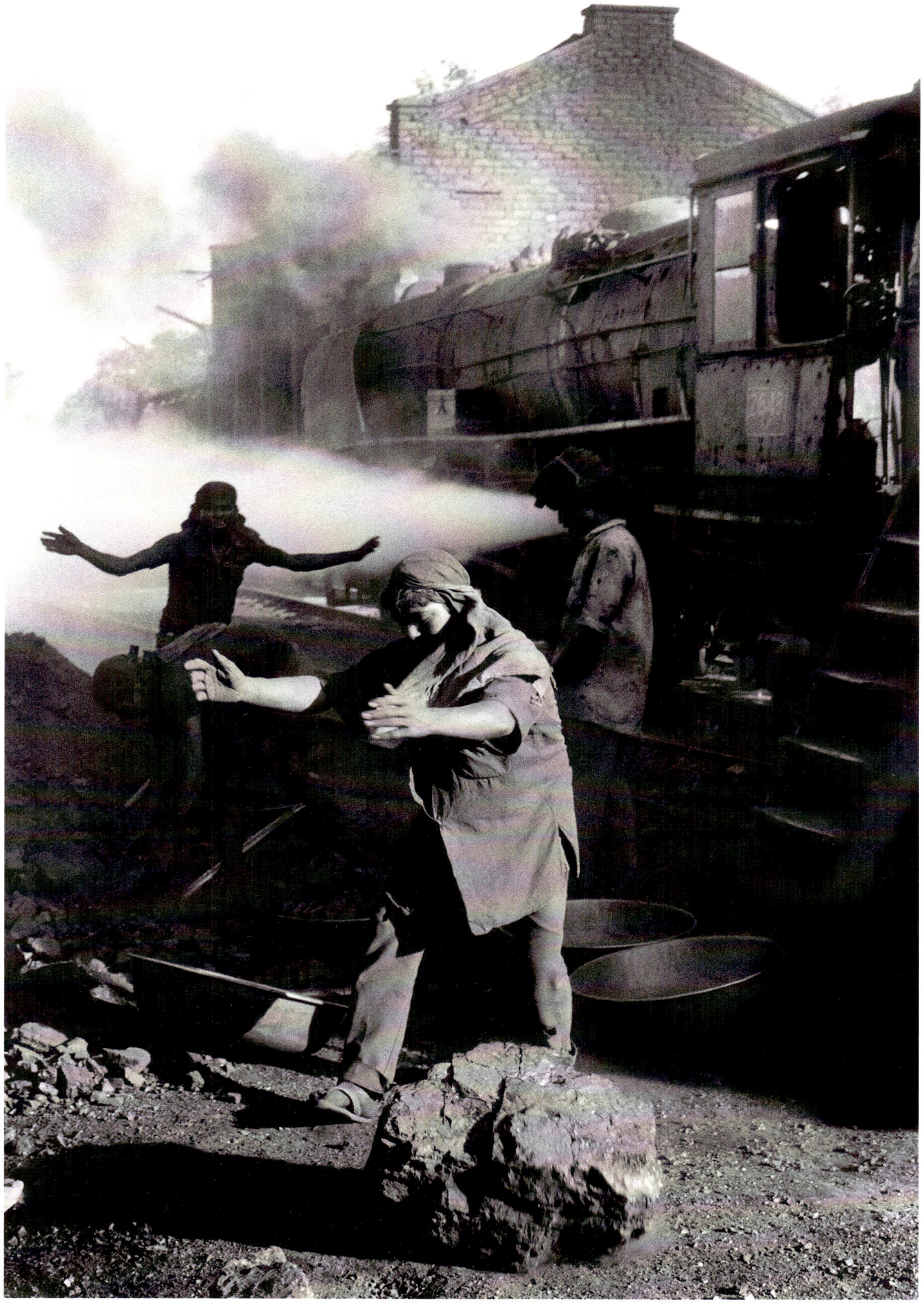

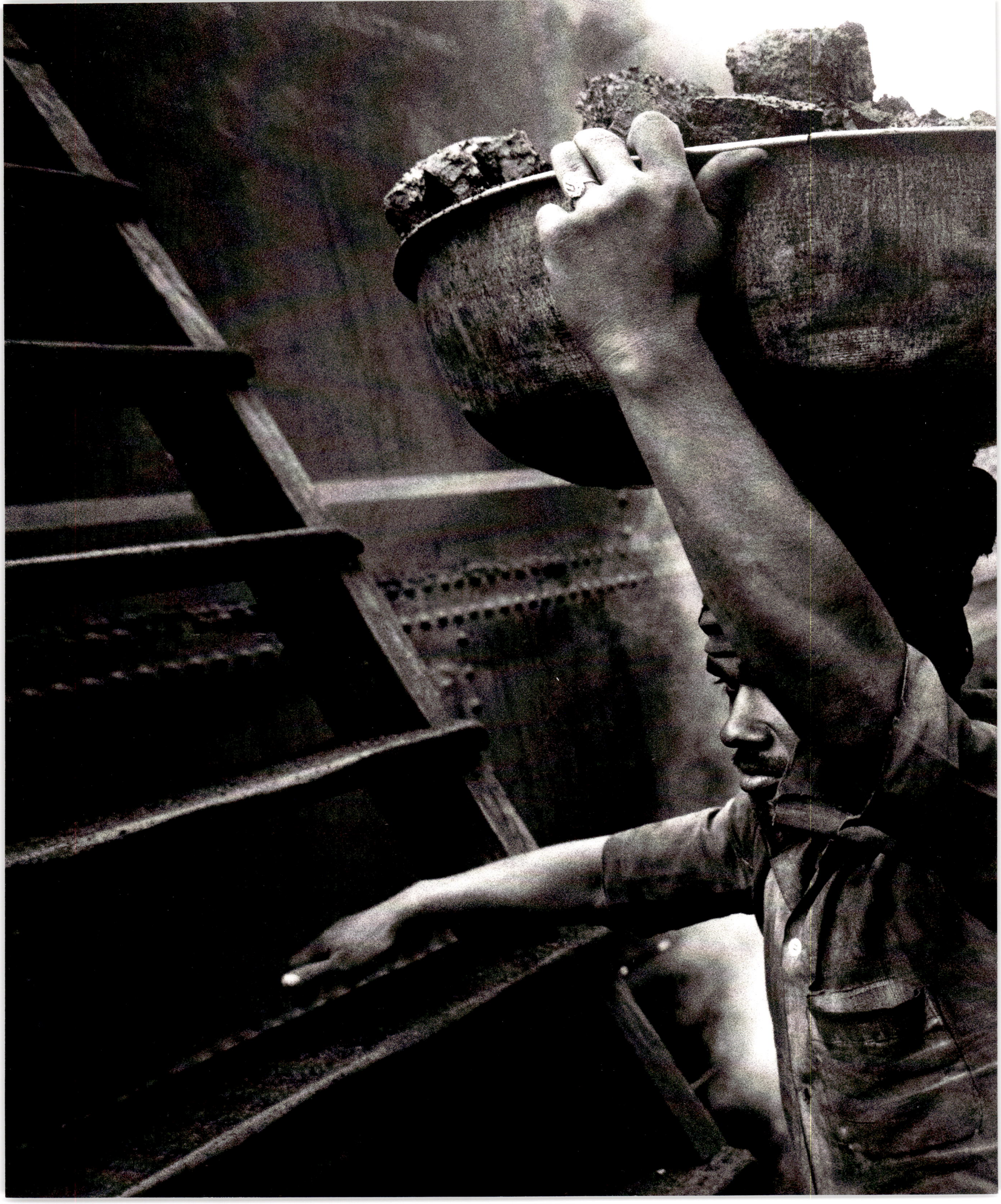

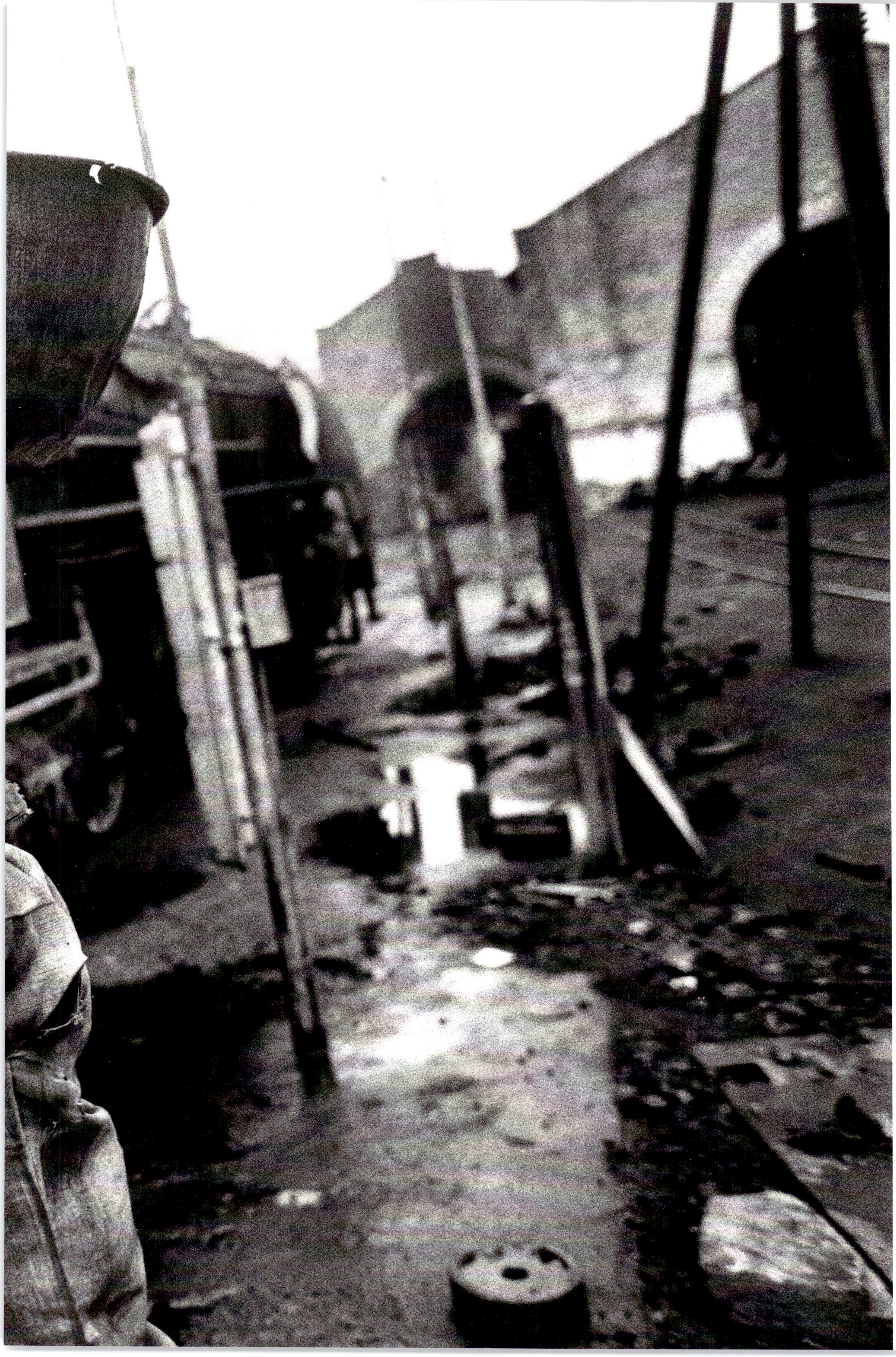

Loading the
engine's coal wagon,
Rana Pratap Nagar,
Rajastan.

following page
Rana Pratap Nagar
loco shed.

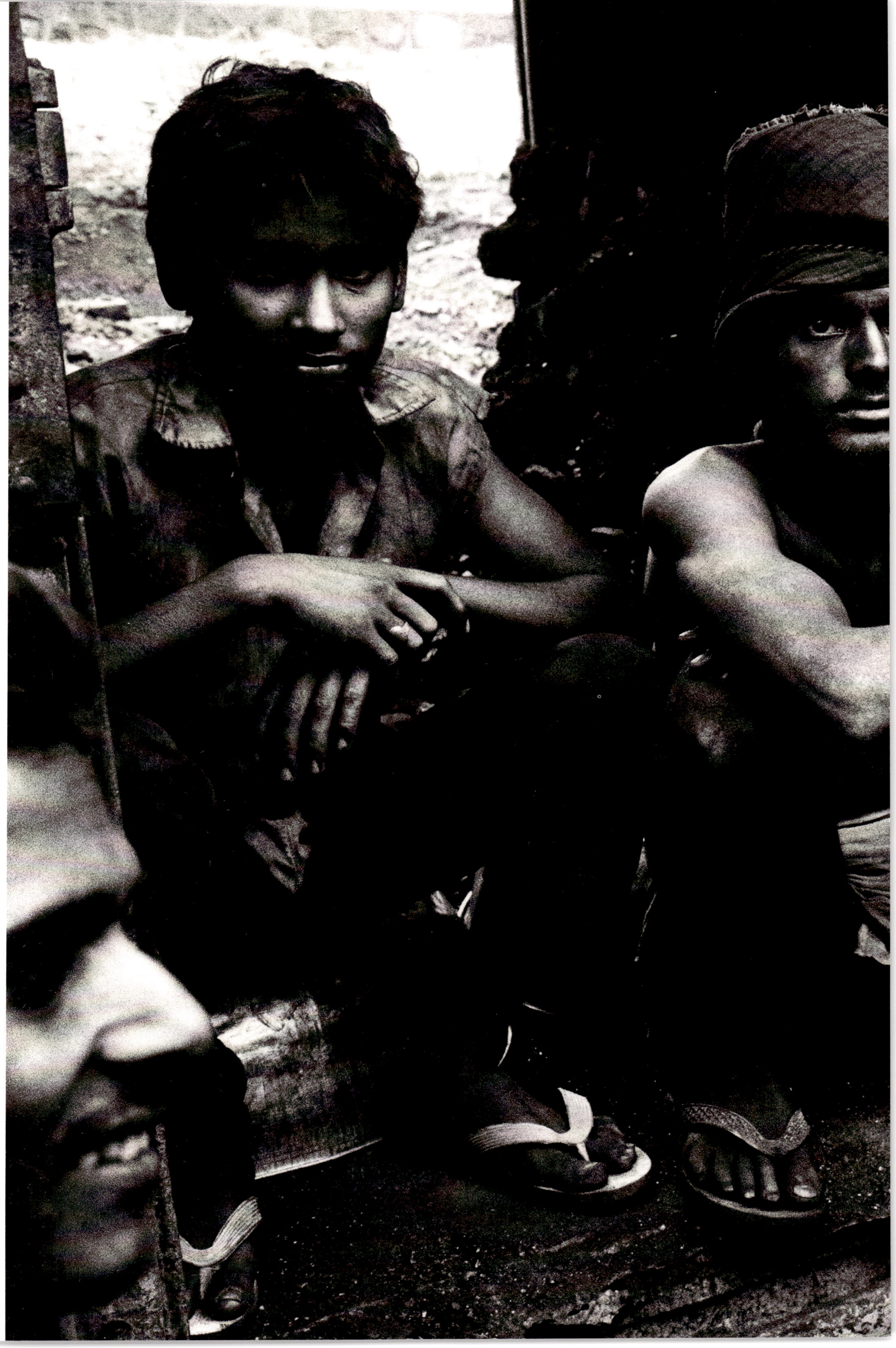

Coal workers
from Bihar State
relaxing during
a 24 hour shift at
Rana Pratap Nagar's
loco shed, Rajastan.

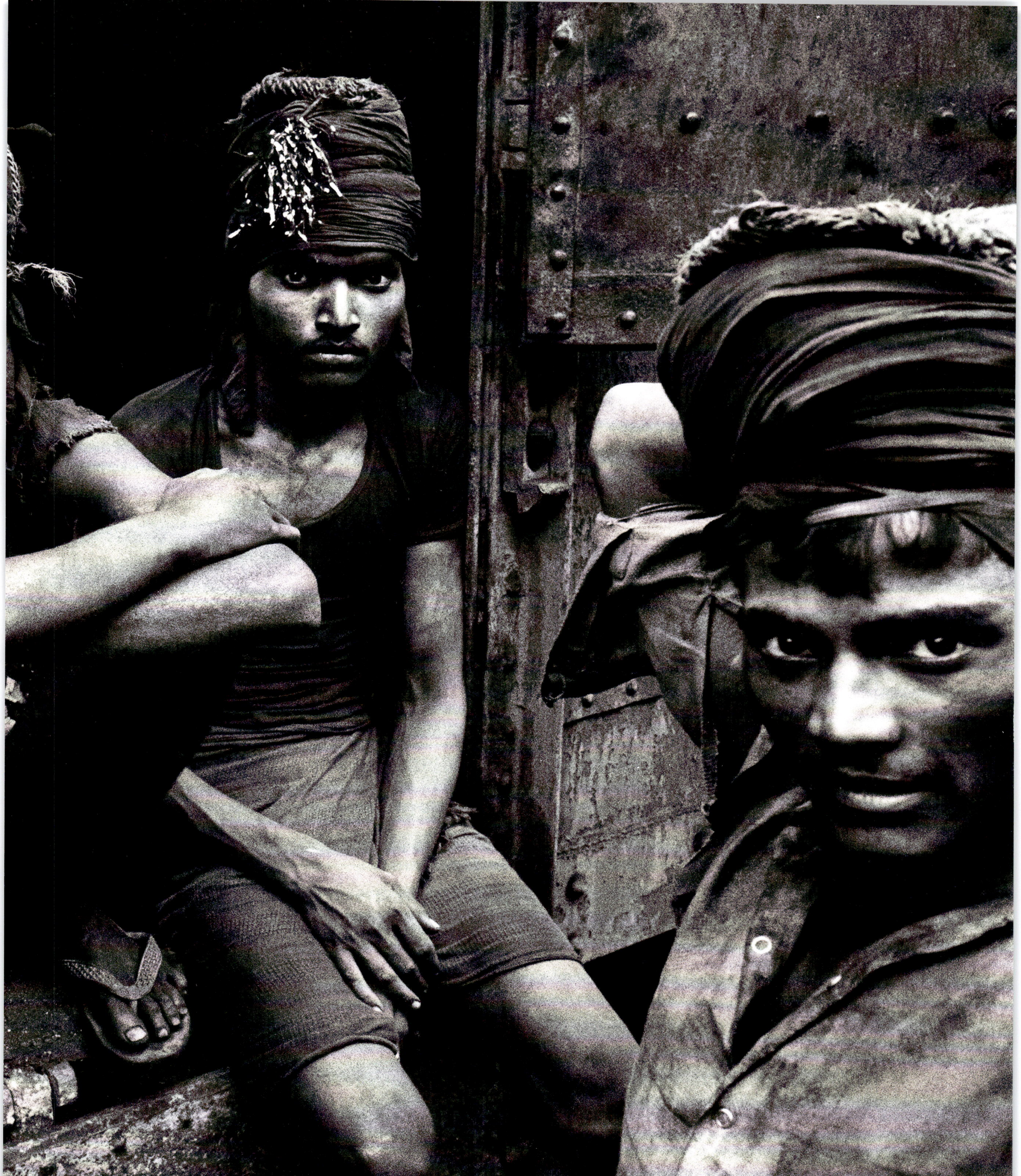

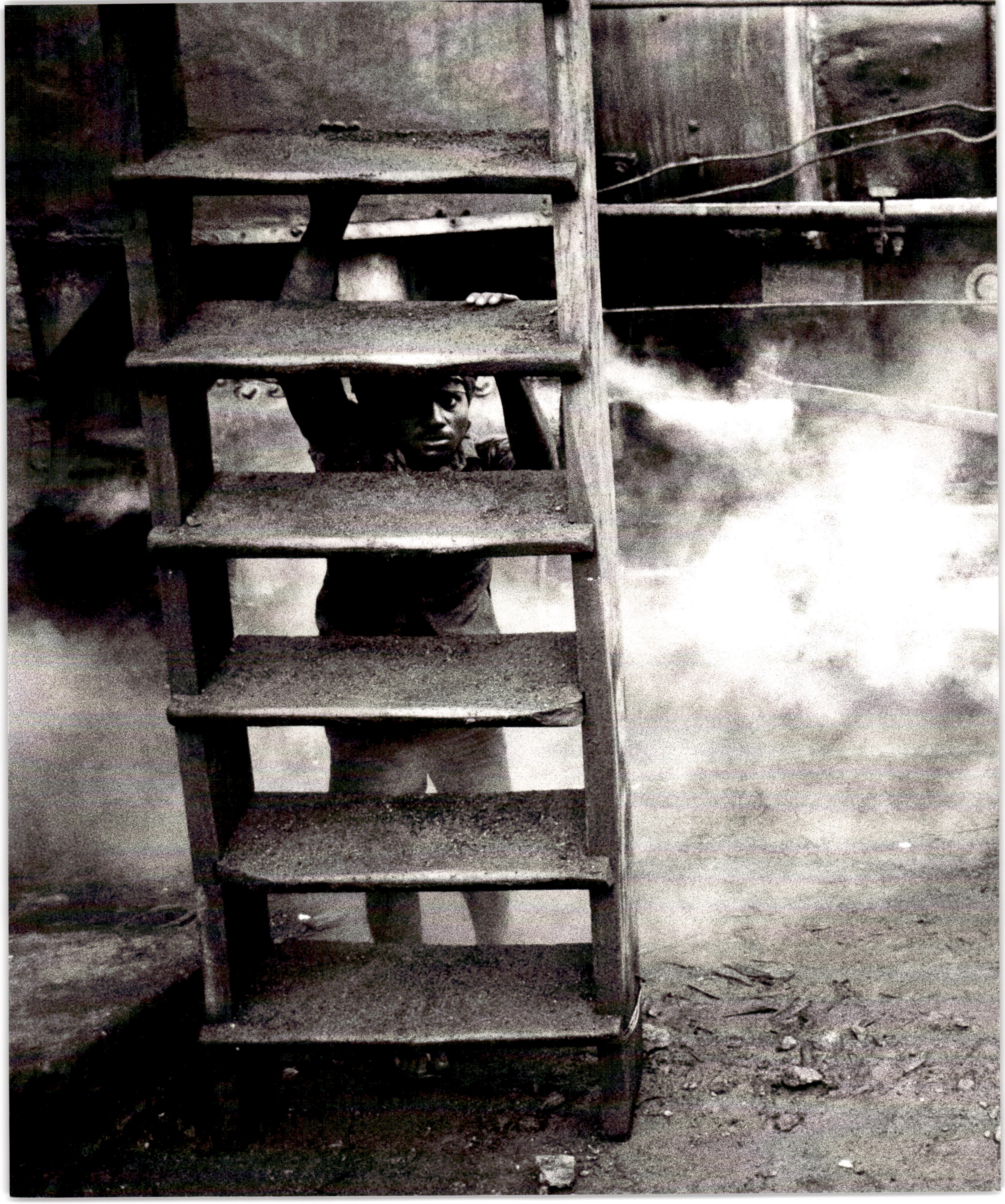

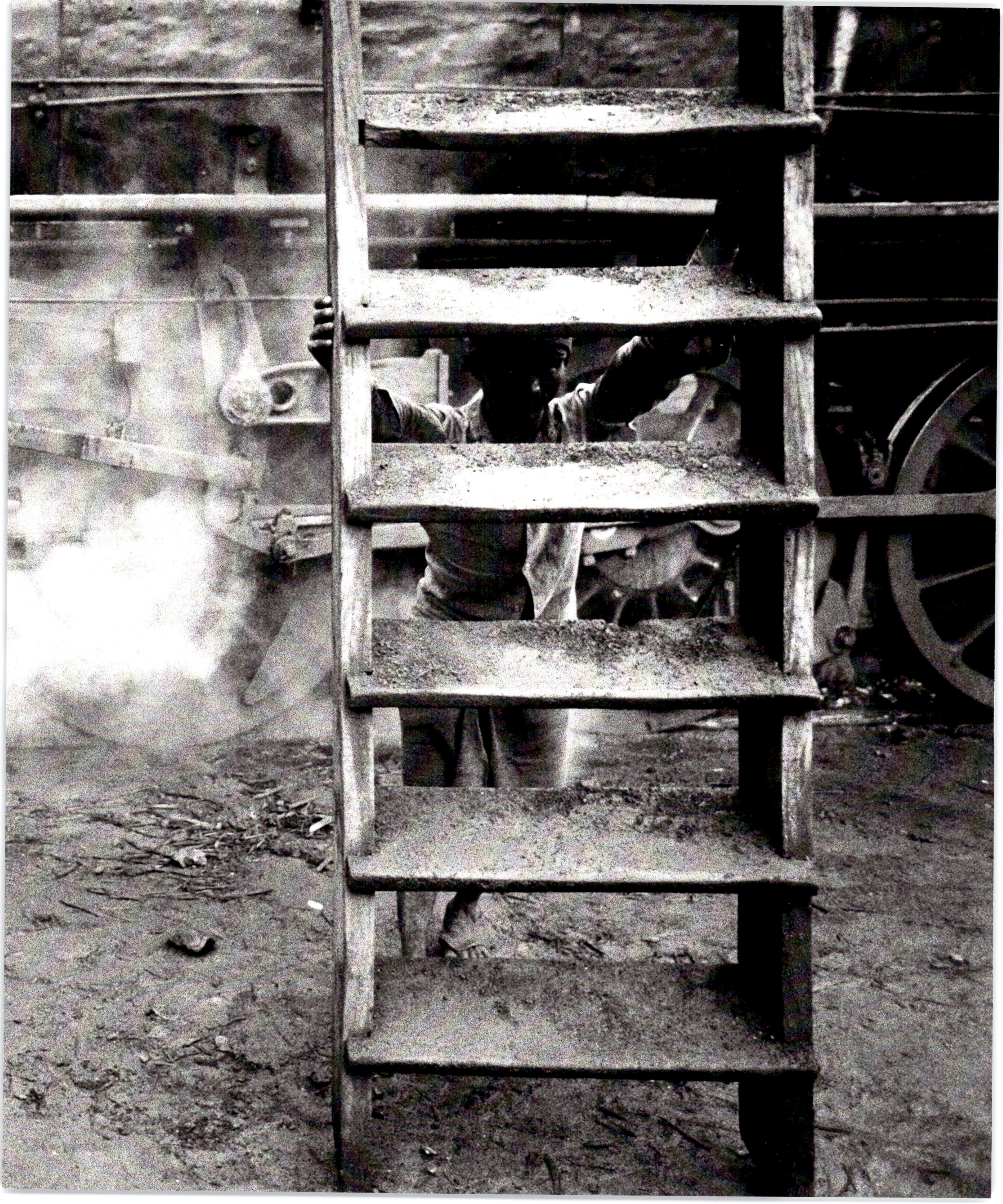

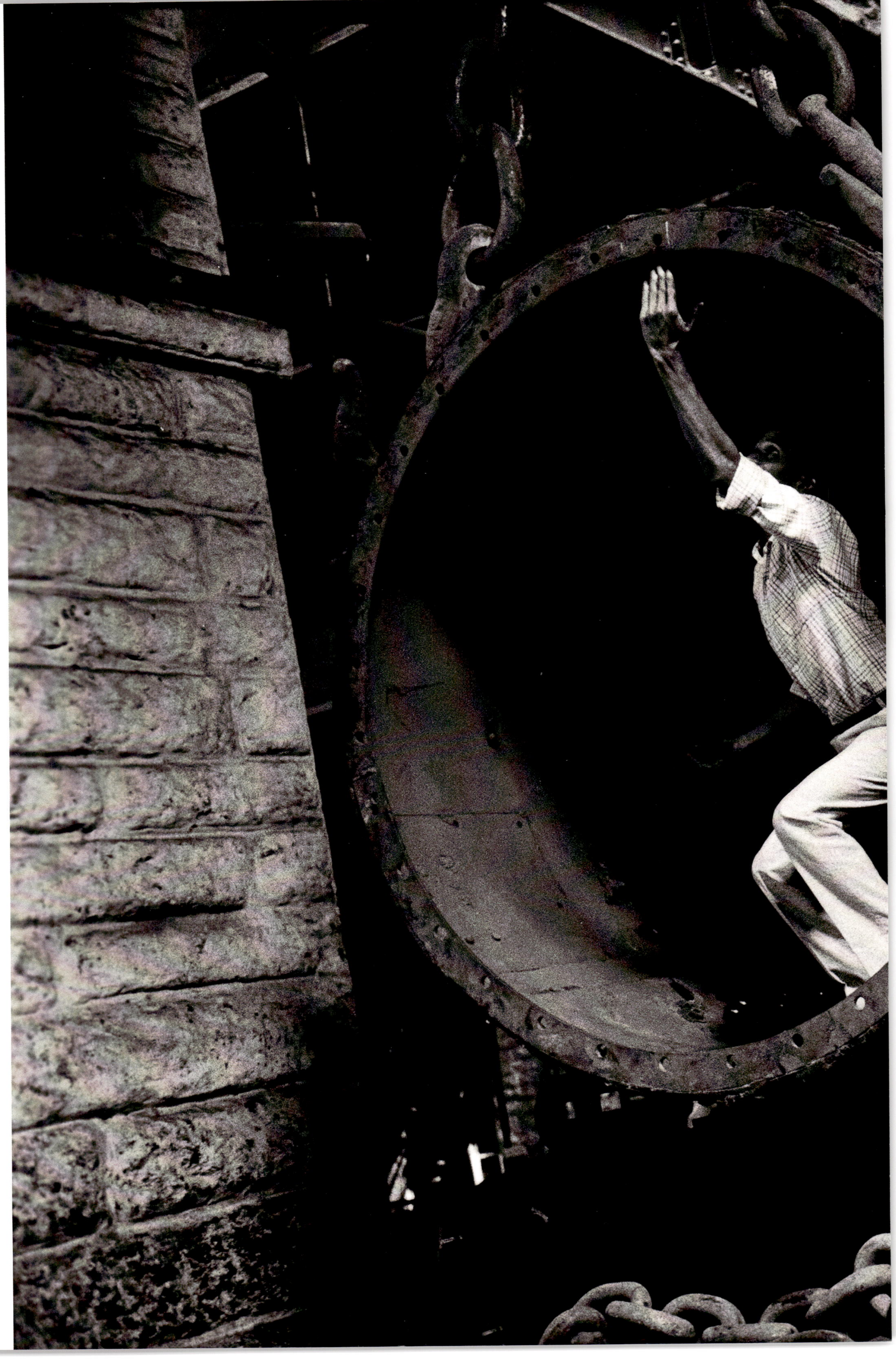

Destroying the
engines for recycling,
Ajmer workshop,
Rajasthan.

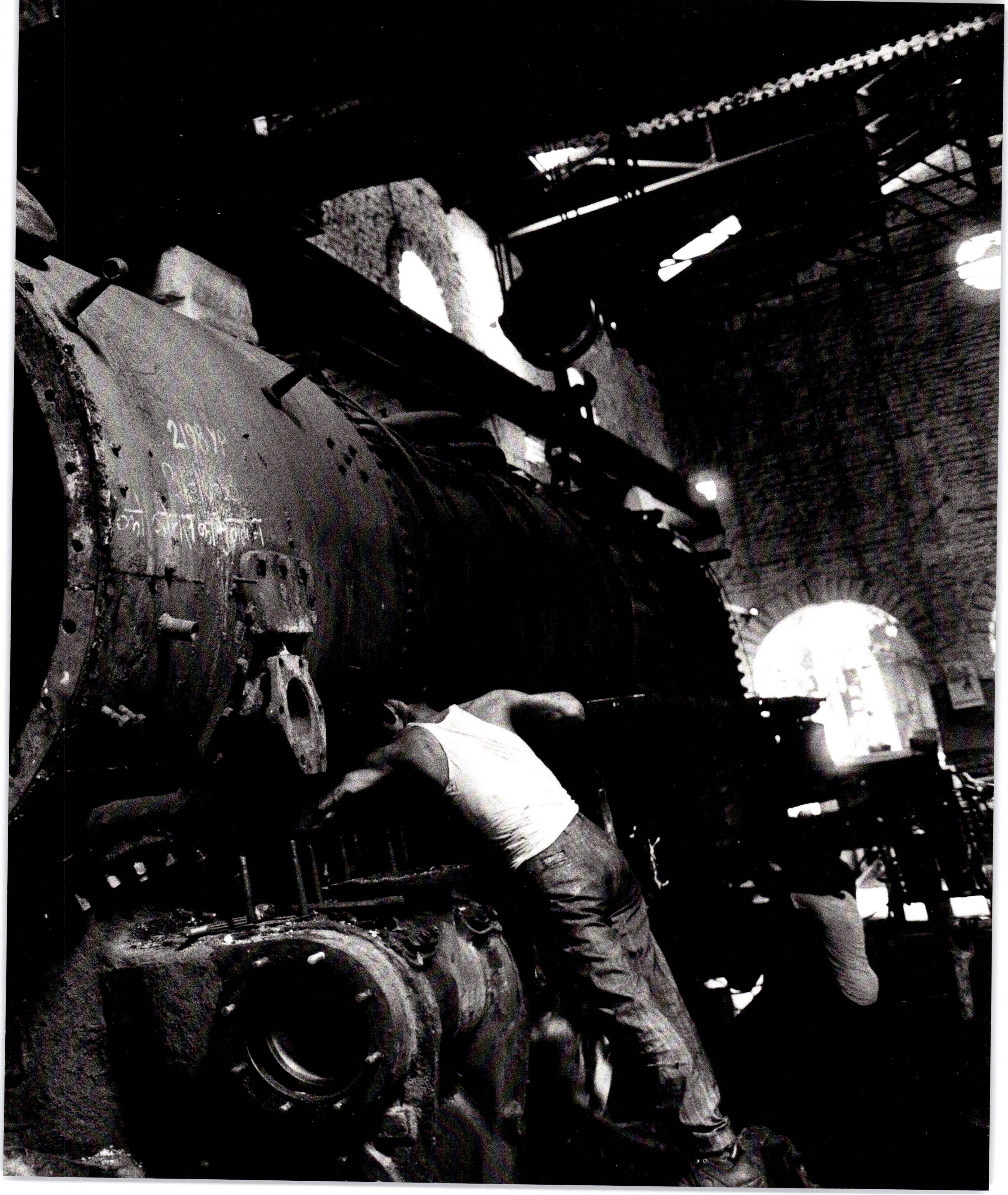

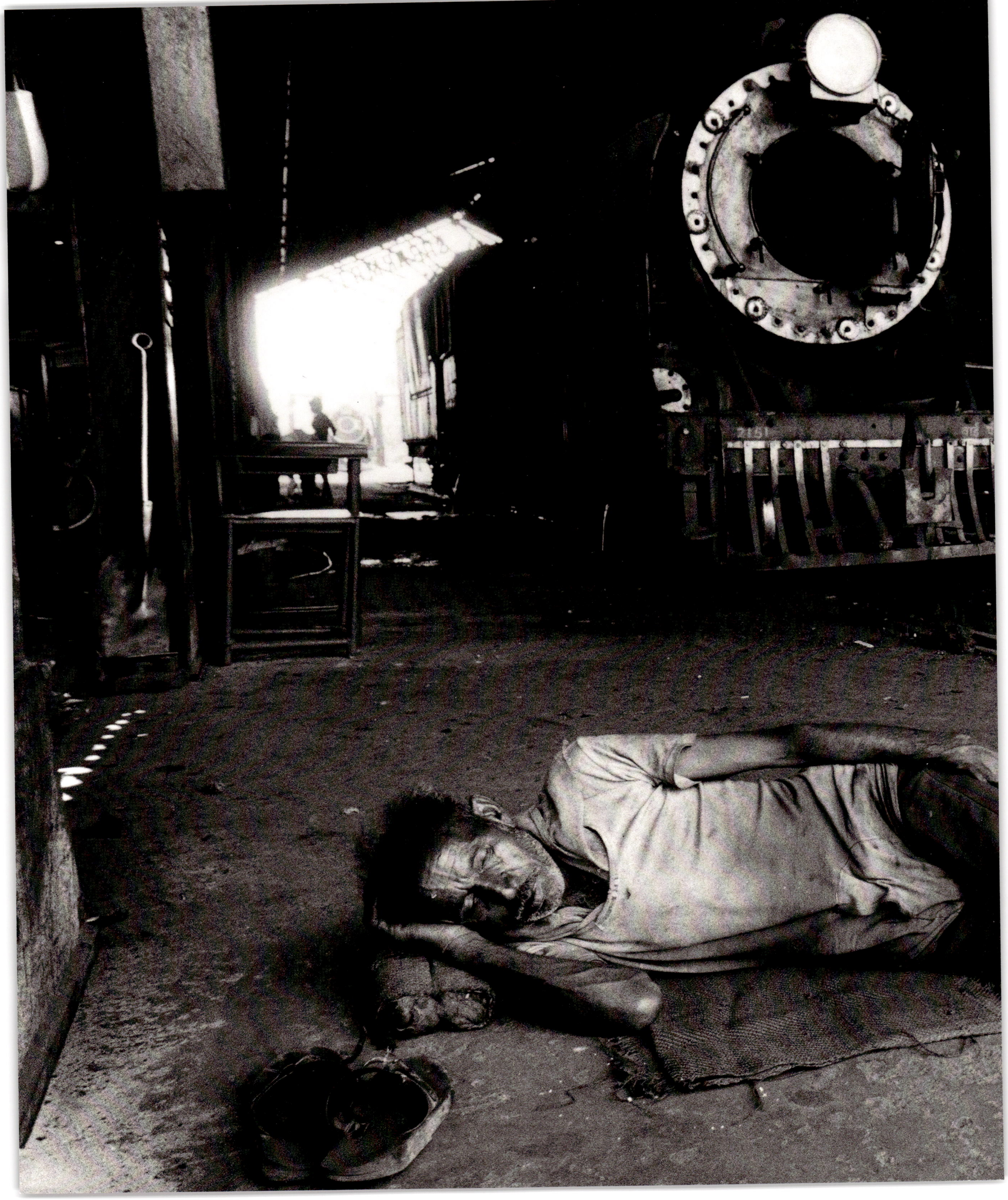

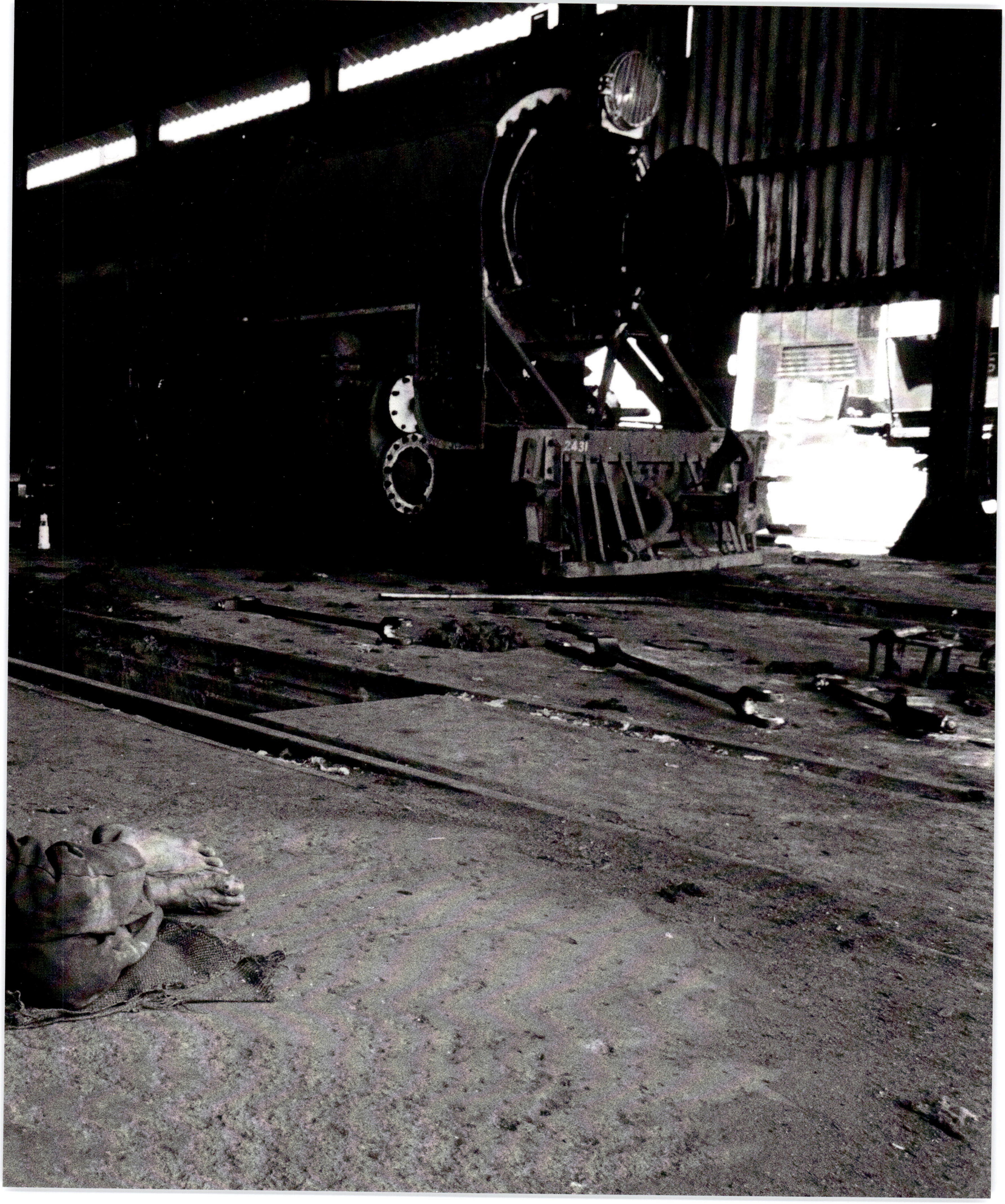

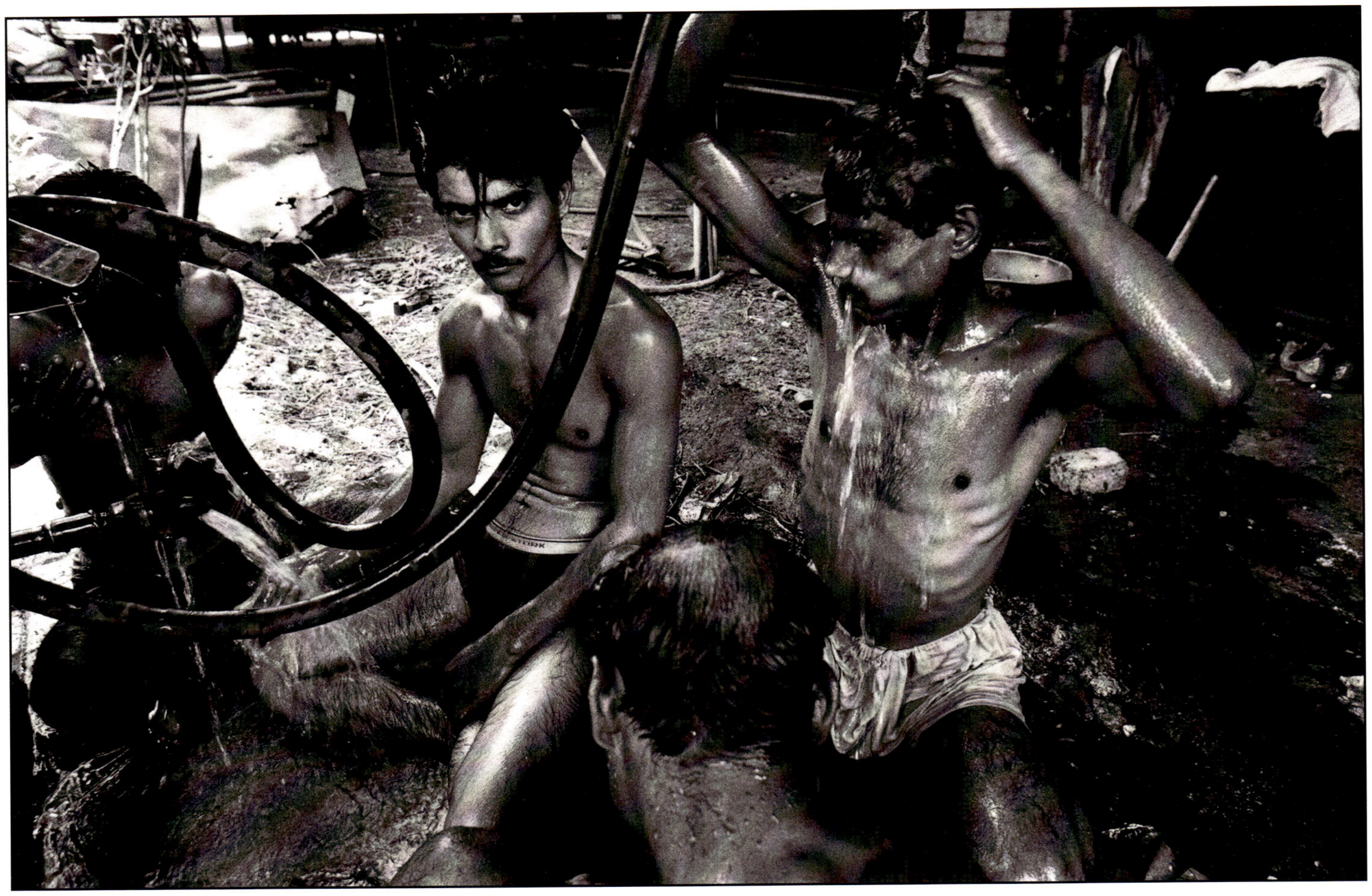

above and opposite page
Having a wash after work at Rana Pratap Nagar loco shed, Rajastan.

previous page
Man sleeps at Sabarati loco shed, Gujarat.

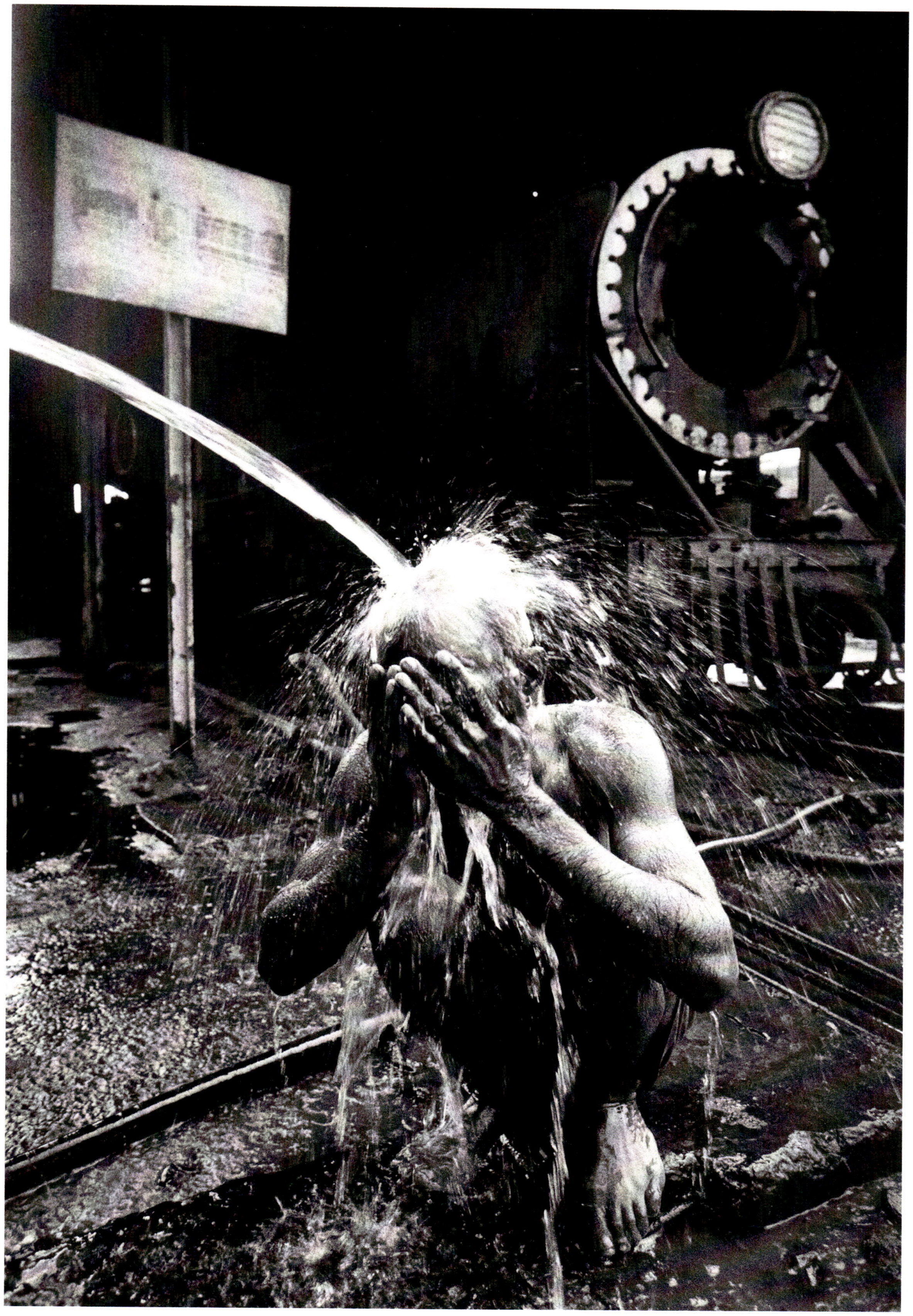

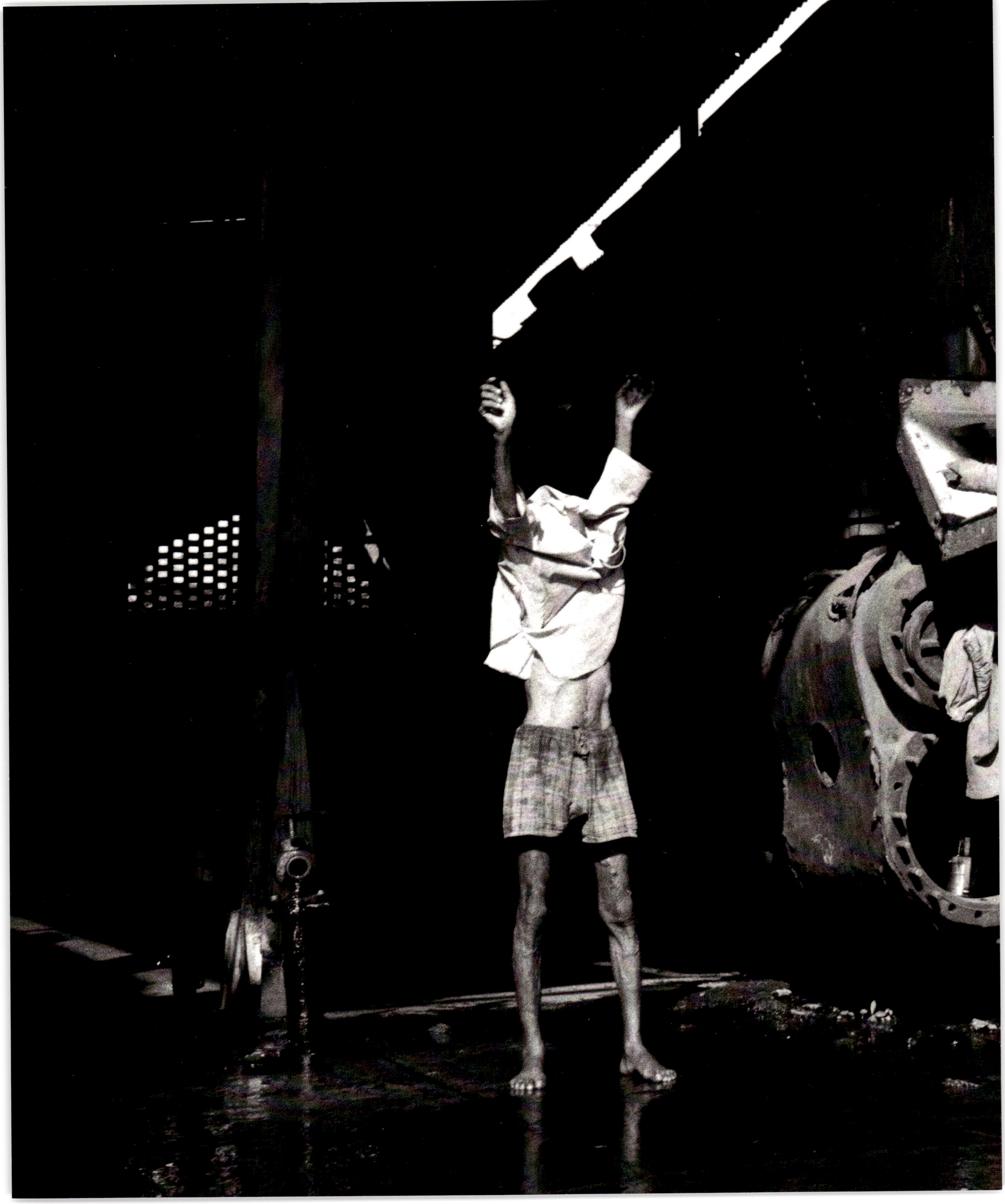

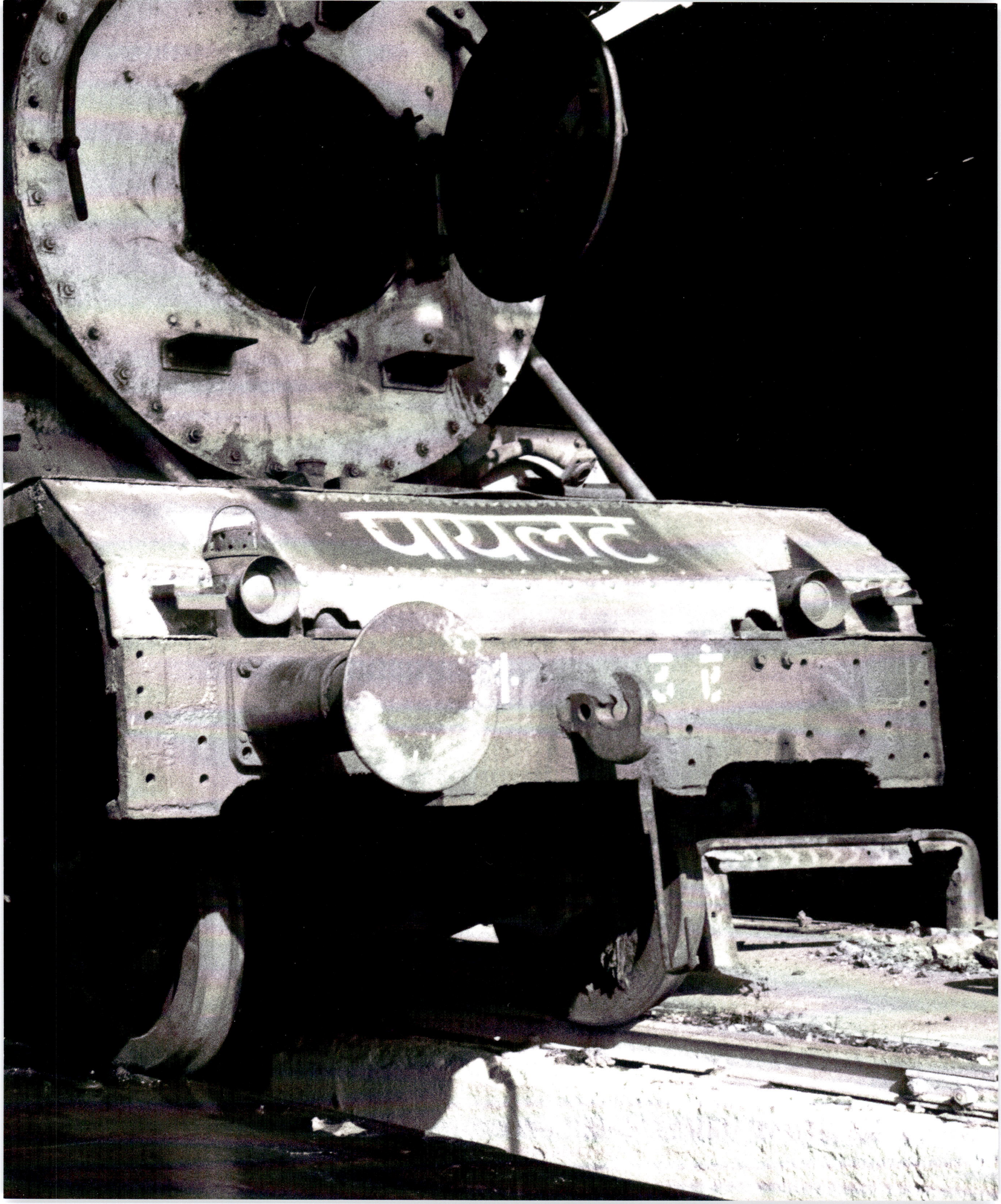
पायलट

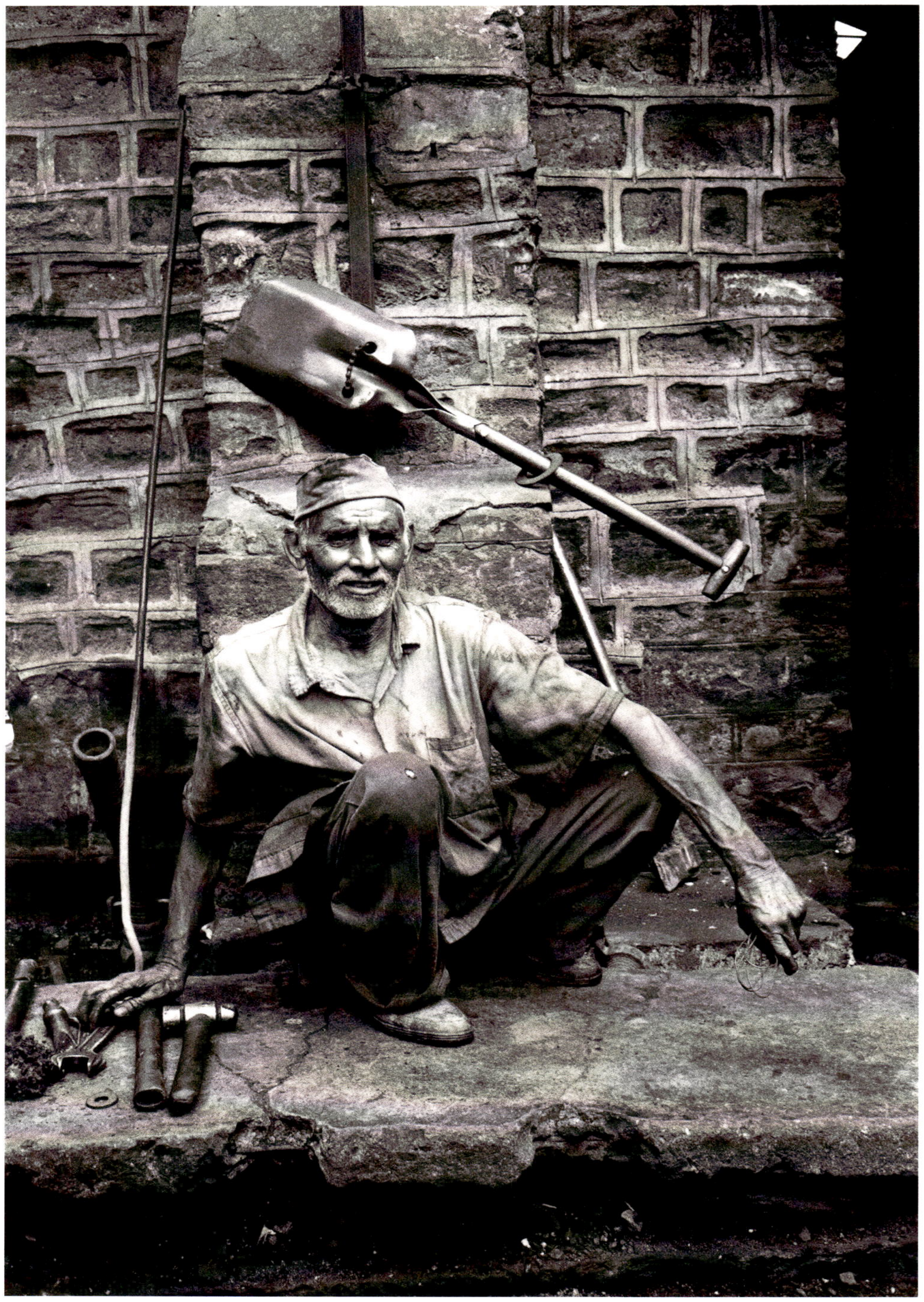

above
A locomotive mechanic, Rana Pratap Nagar, Rajastan.
opposite page
A boiler mechanic at the loco workshop in Ajmer, Rajastan.
previous page
Man dressing after washing, Moradabad loco shed, Uttar Pradesh.

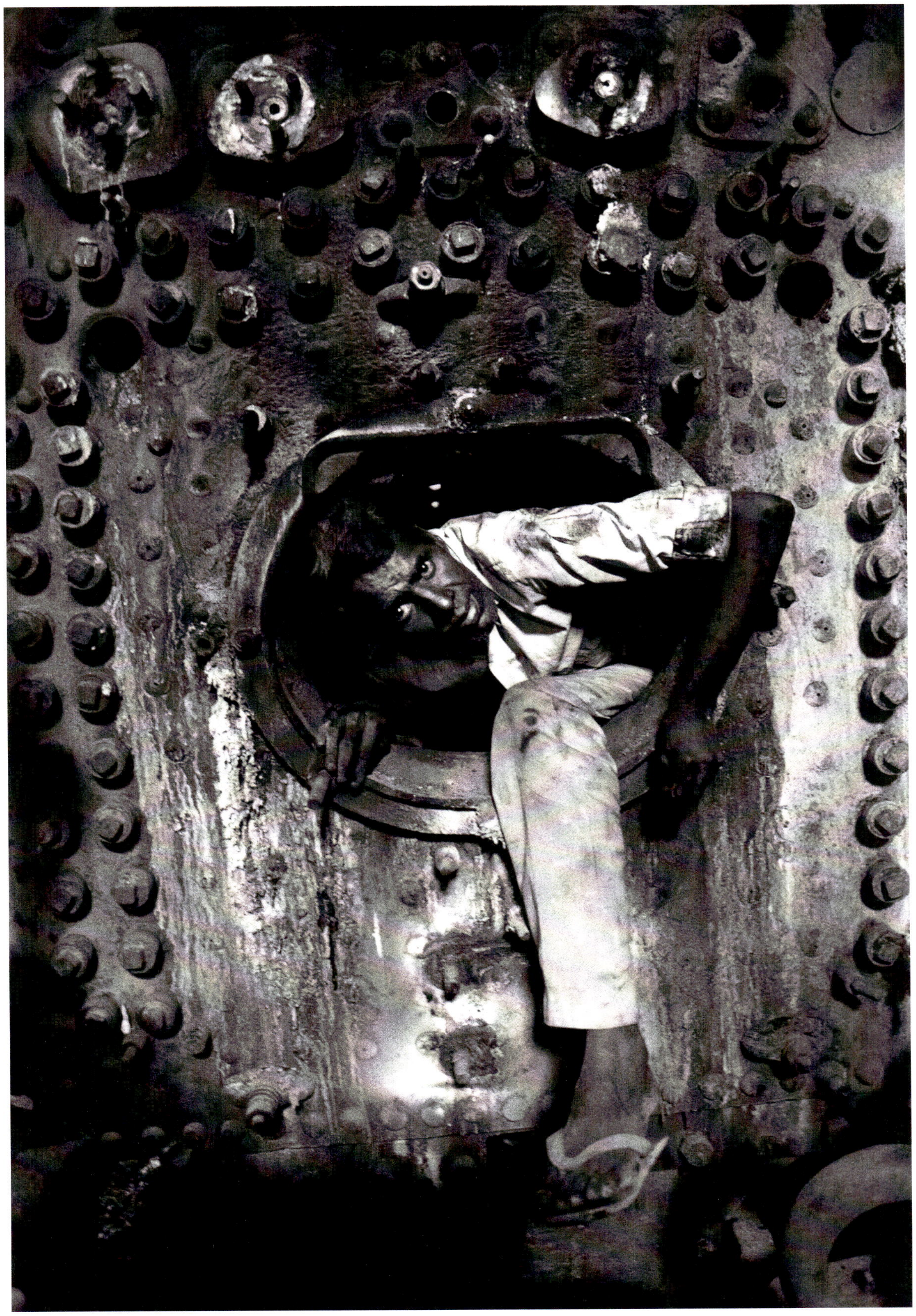

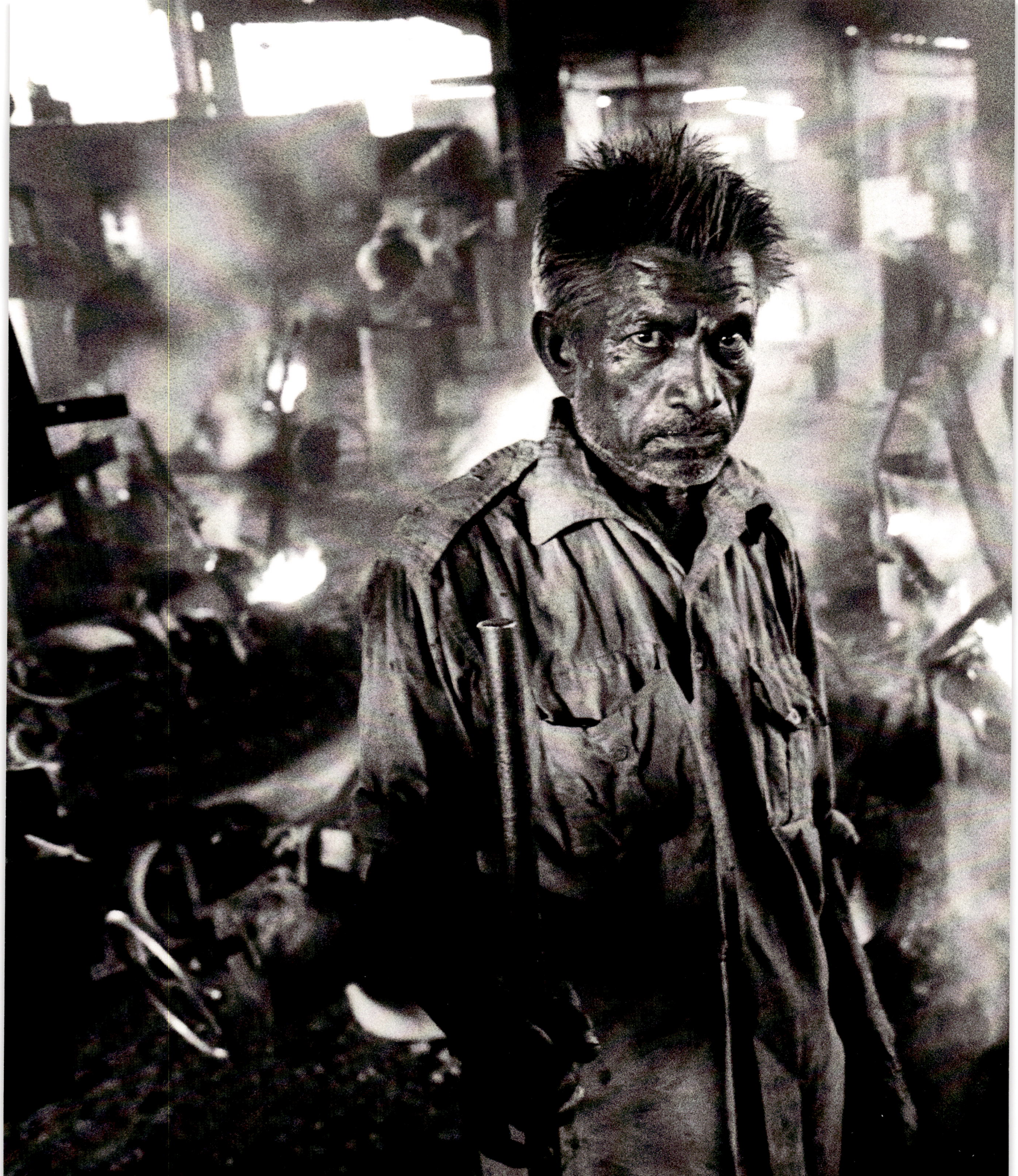

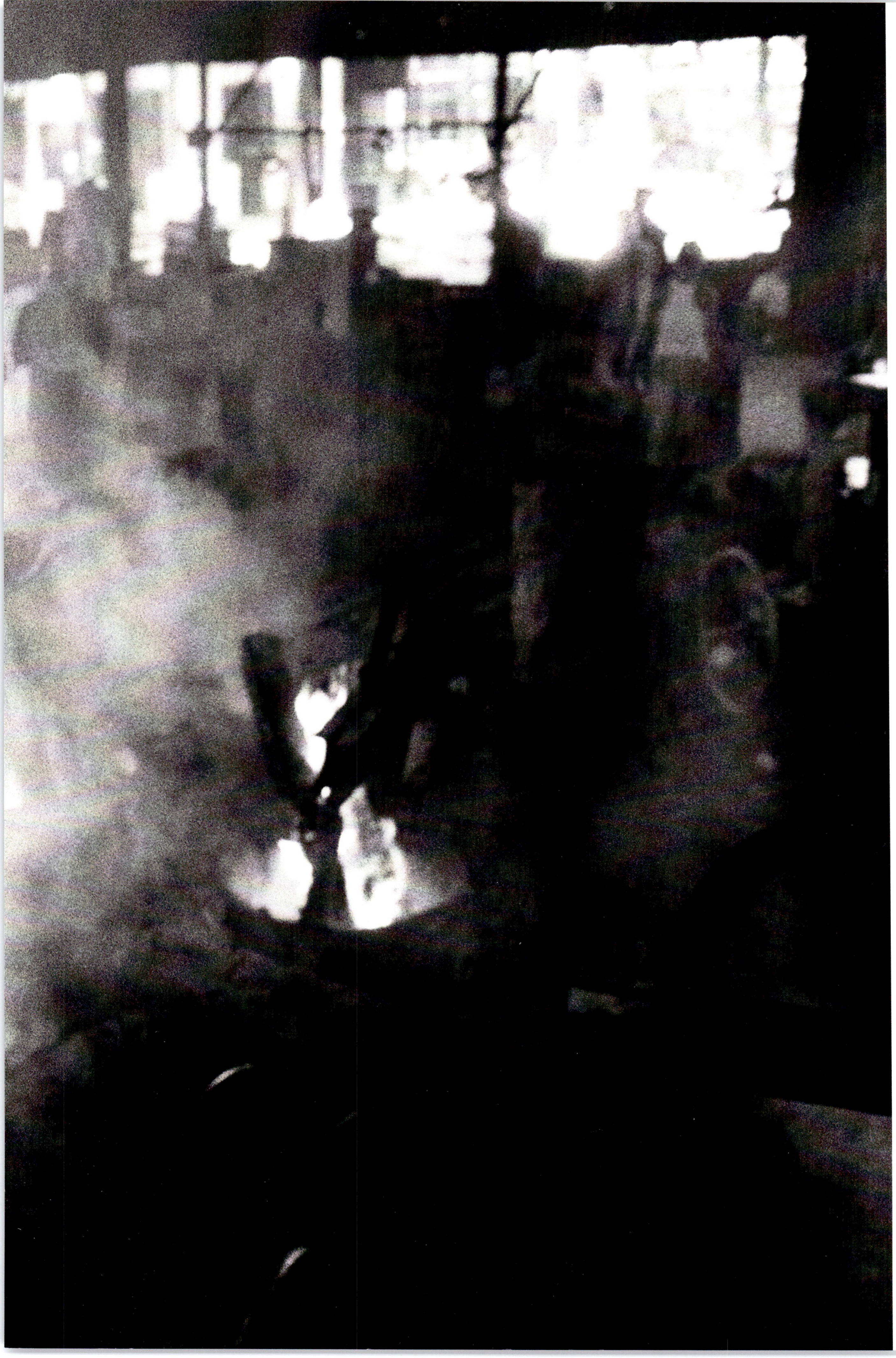

Worker in the
iron melting shed,
for steam loco parts.
Ajmer steam loco
workshop, Rajastan.

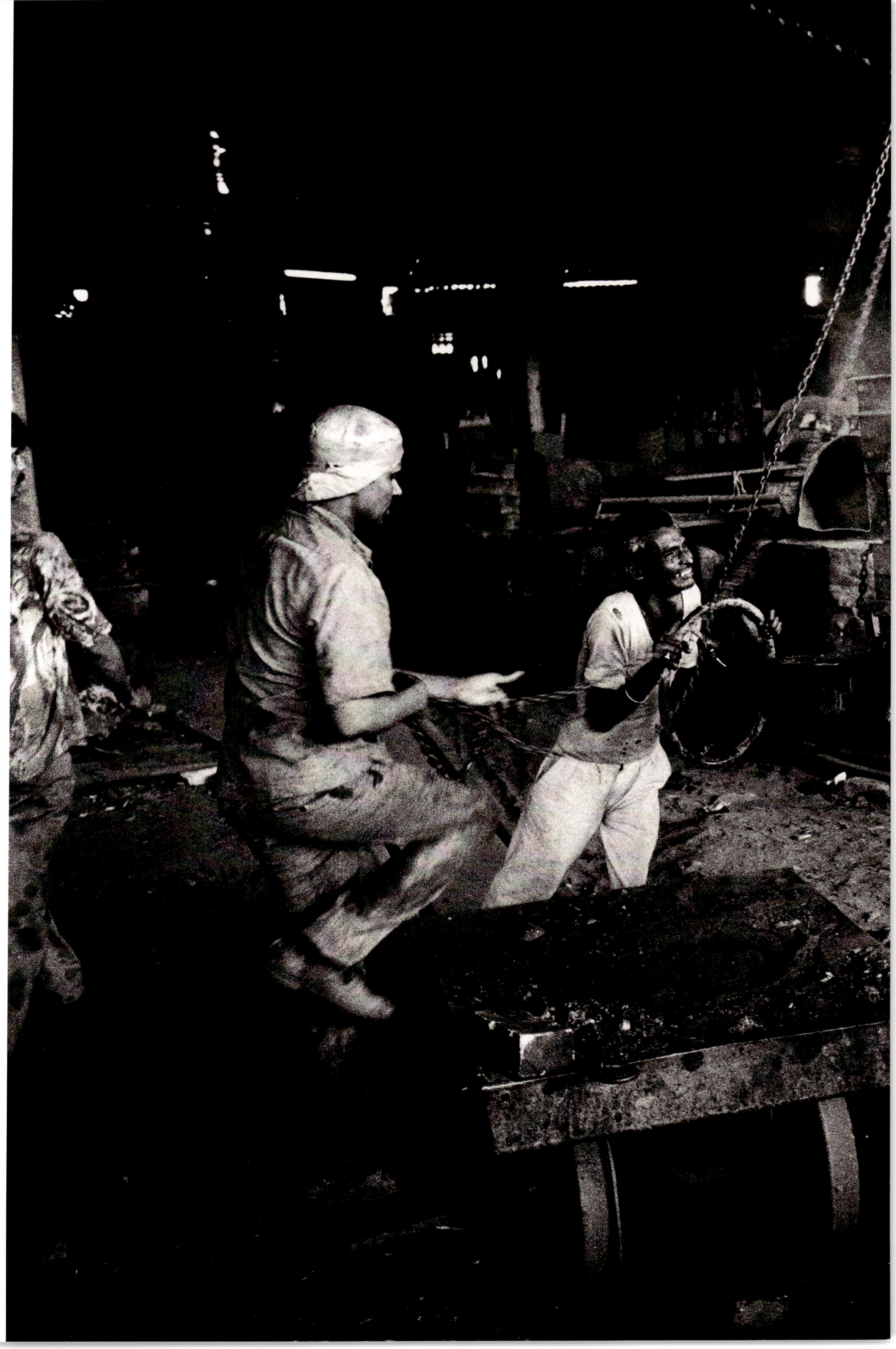

Workers making iron brake pads from moulds at Ajmer's steam loco workshop, Rajastan.

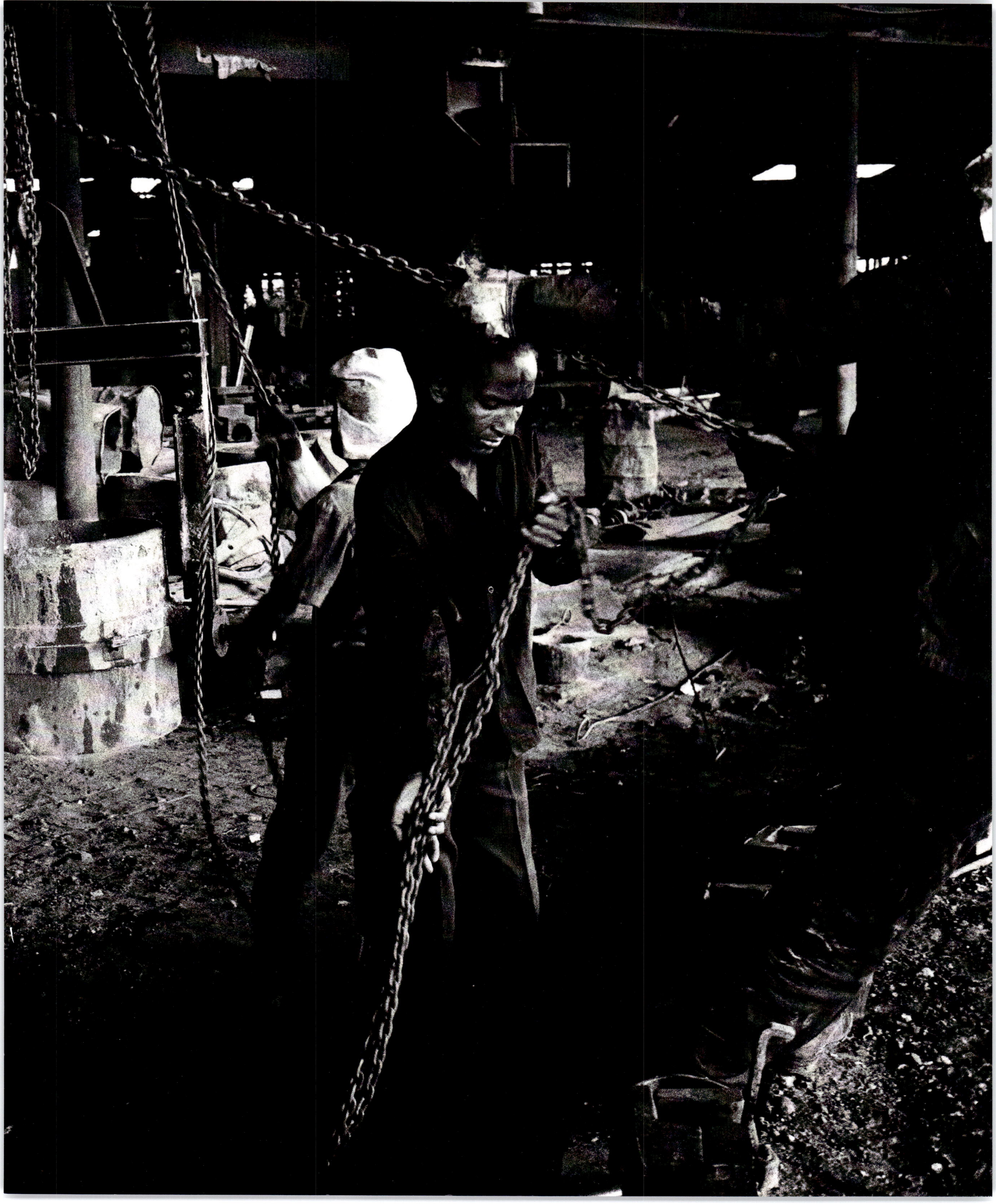

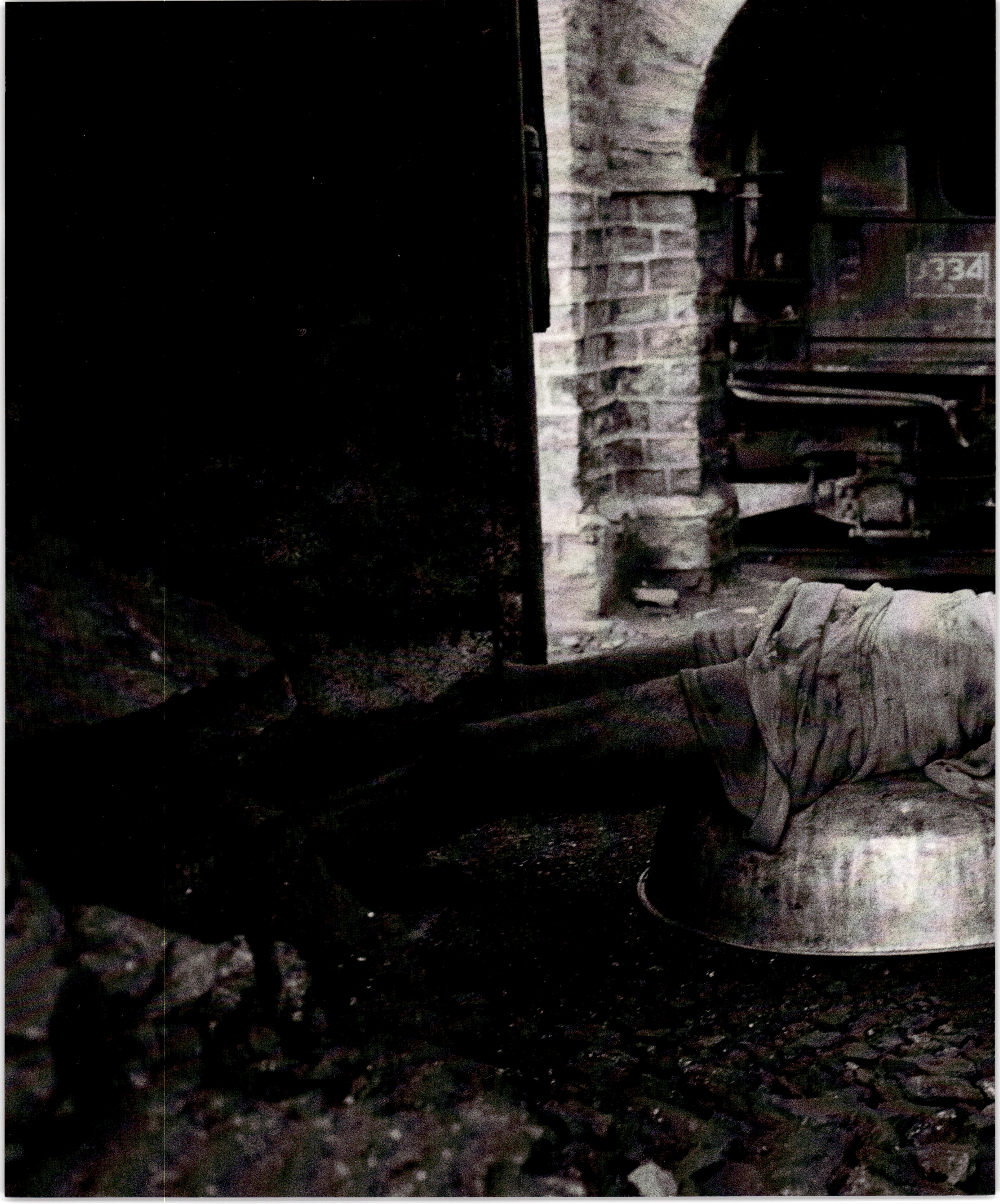

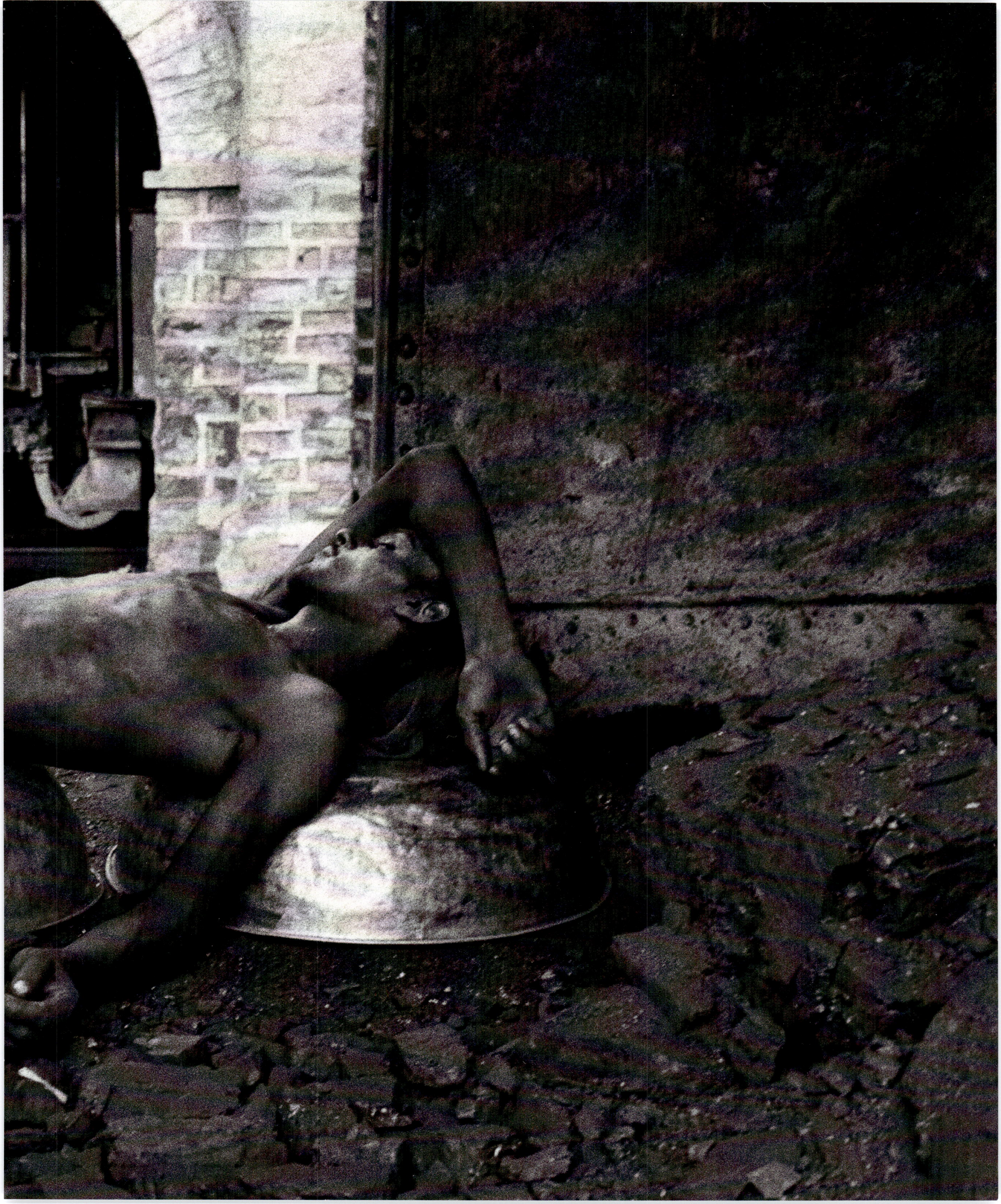

previous page
An exhausted worker sleeps inside a coal wagon,
Rana Pratap Nagar, Rajastan.

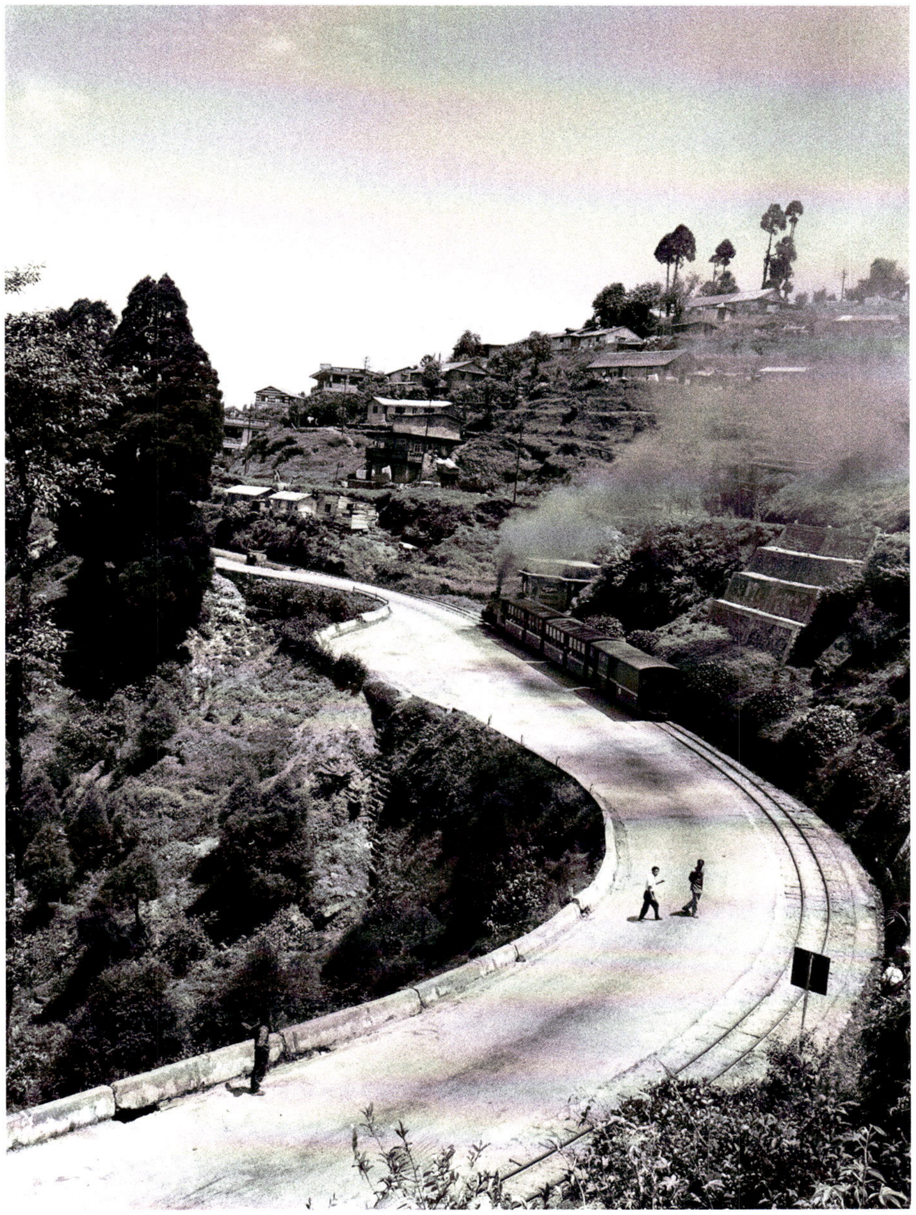

The 'toy train' travelling across the Himalayan foothills towards Darjeeling, West Bengal.

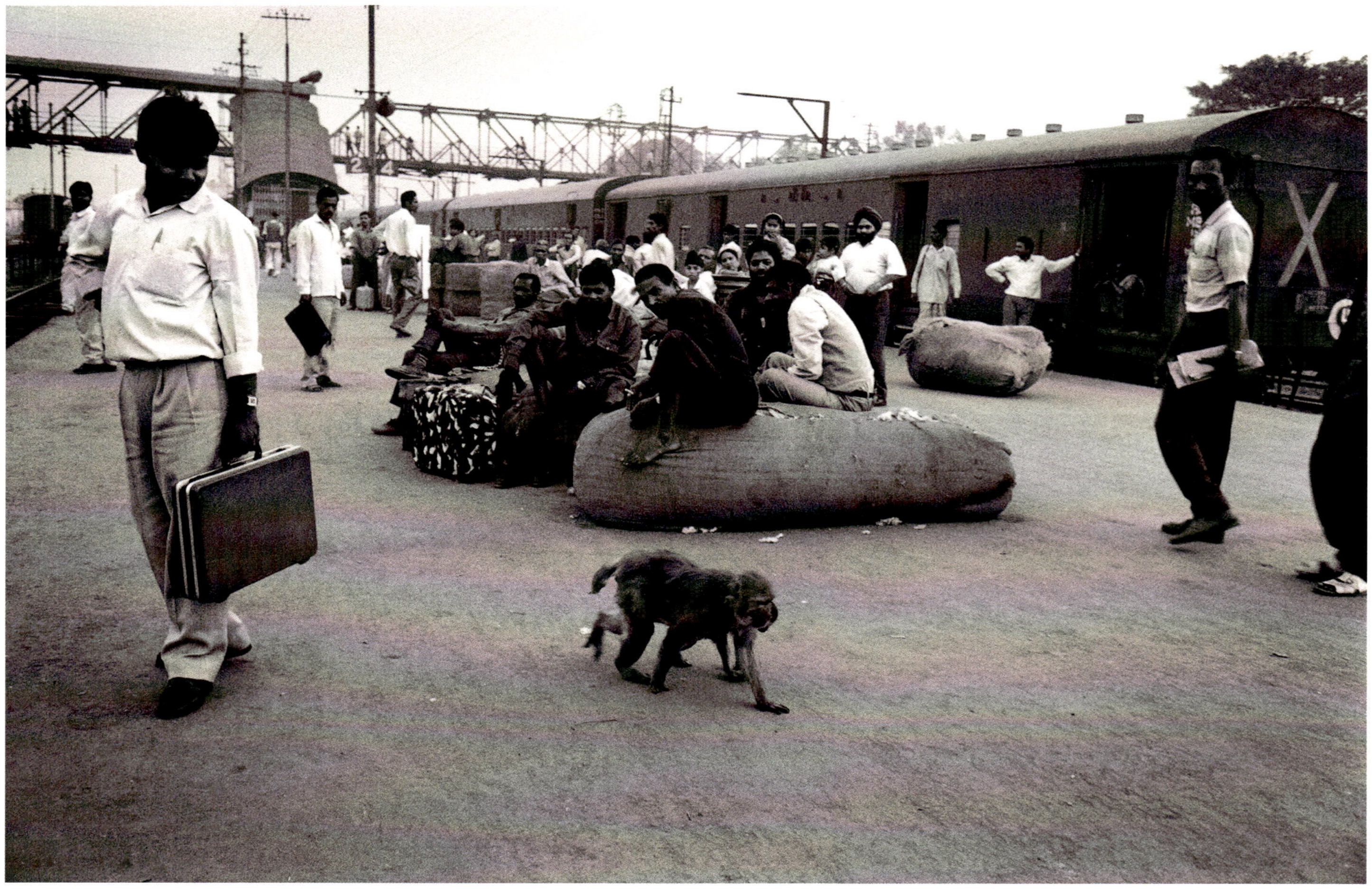

Moradabad Station, Uttar Pradesh.

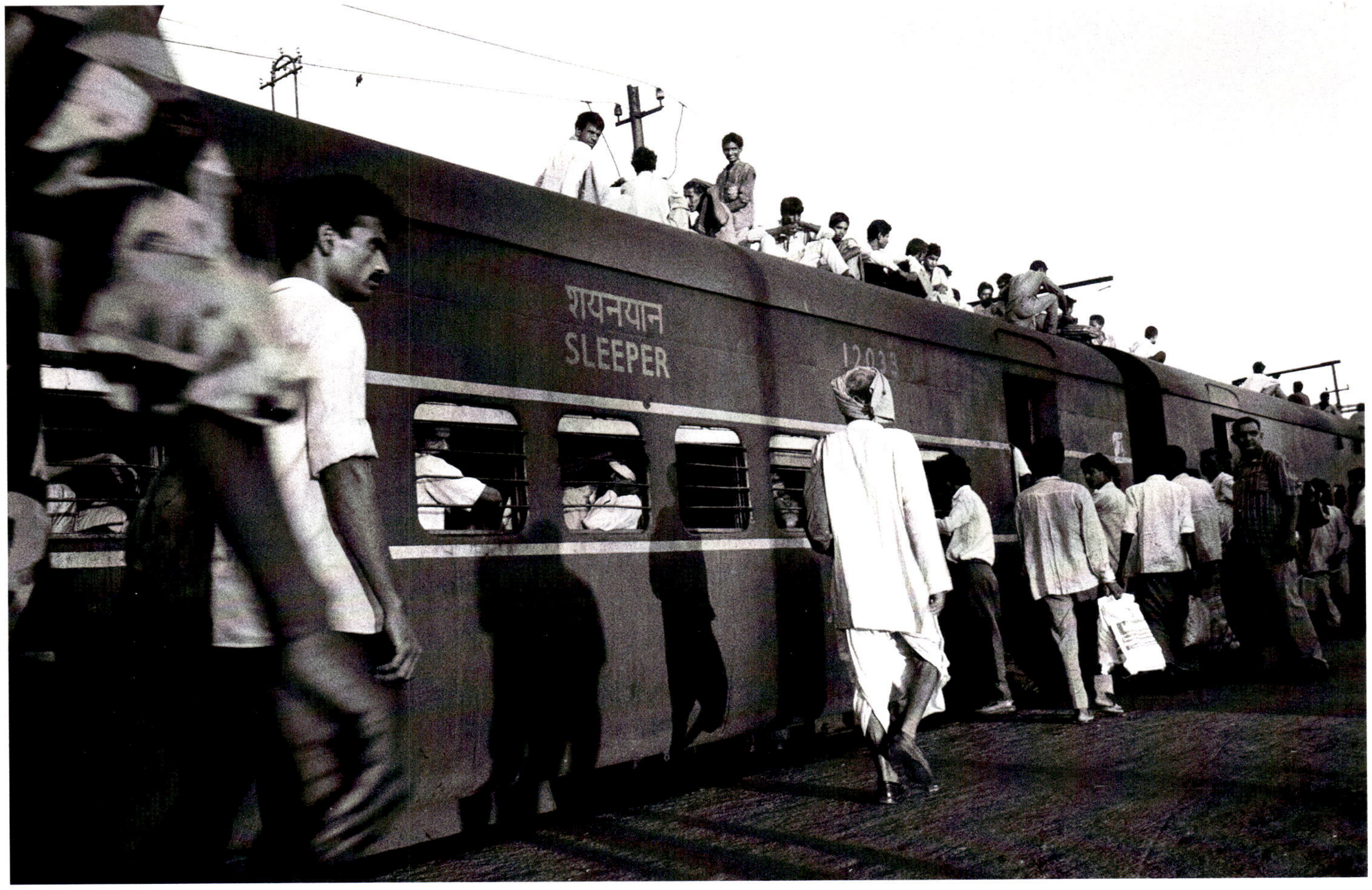

A crowded passenger train at Moradabad Station, Uttar Pradesh.

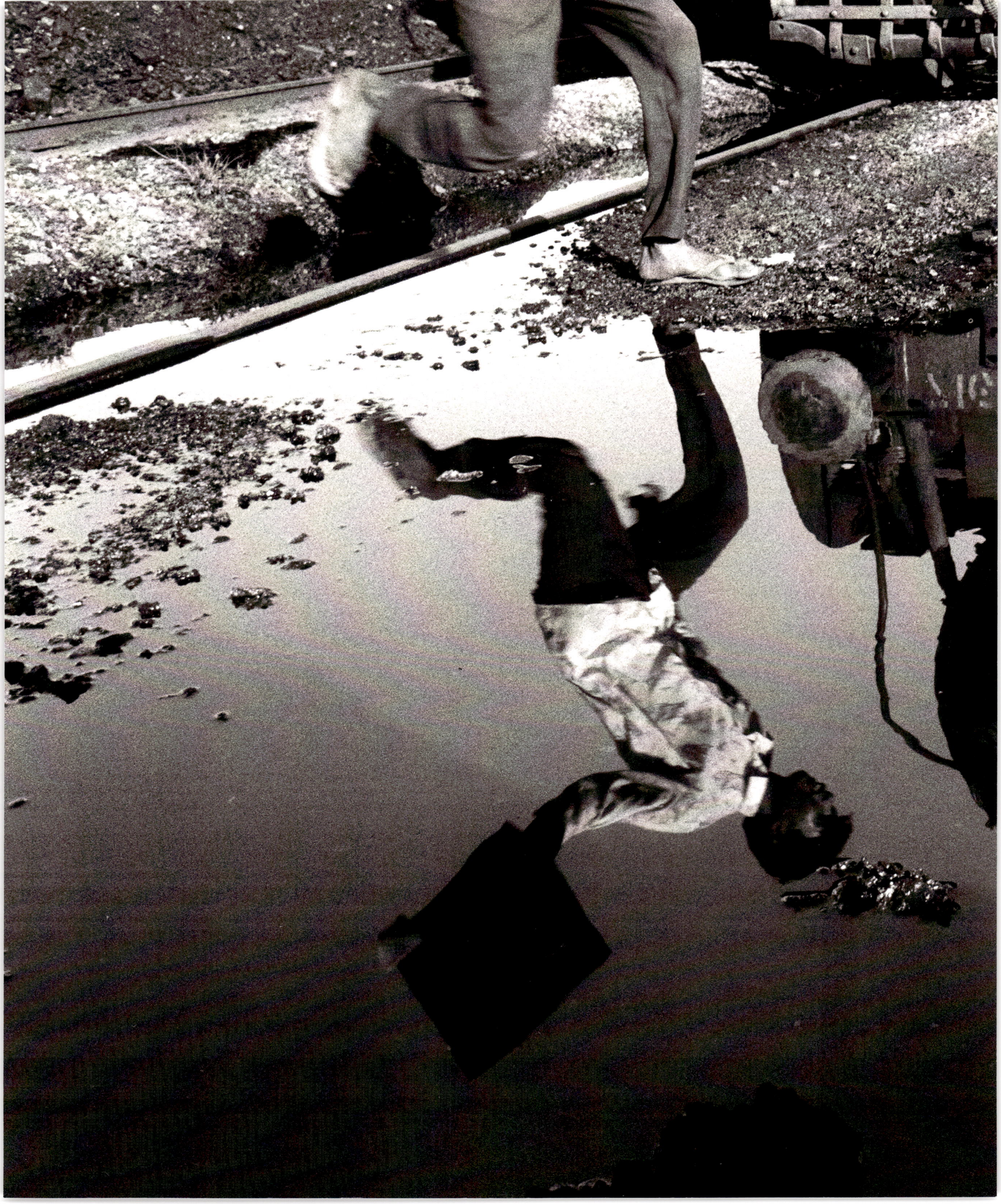

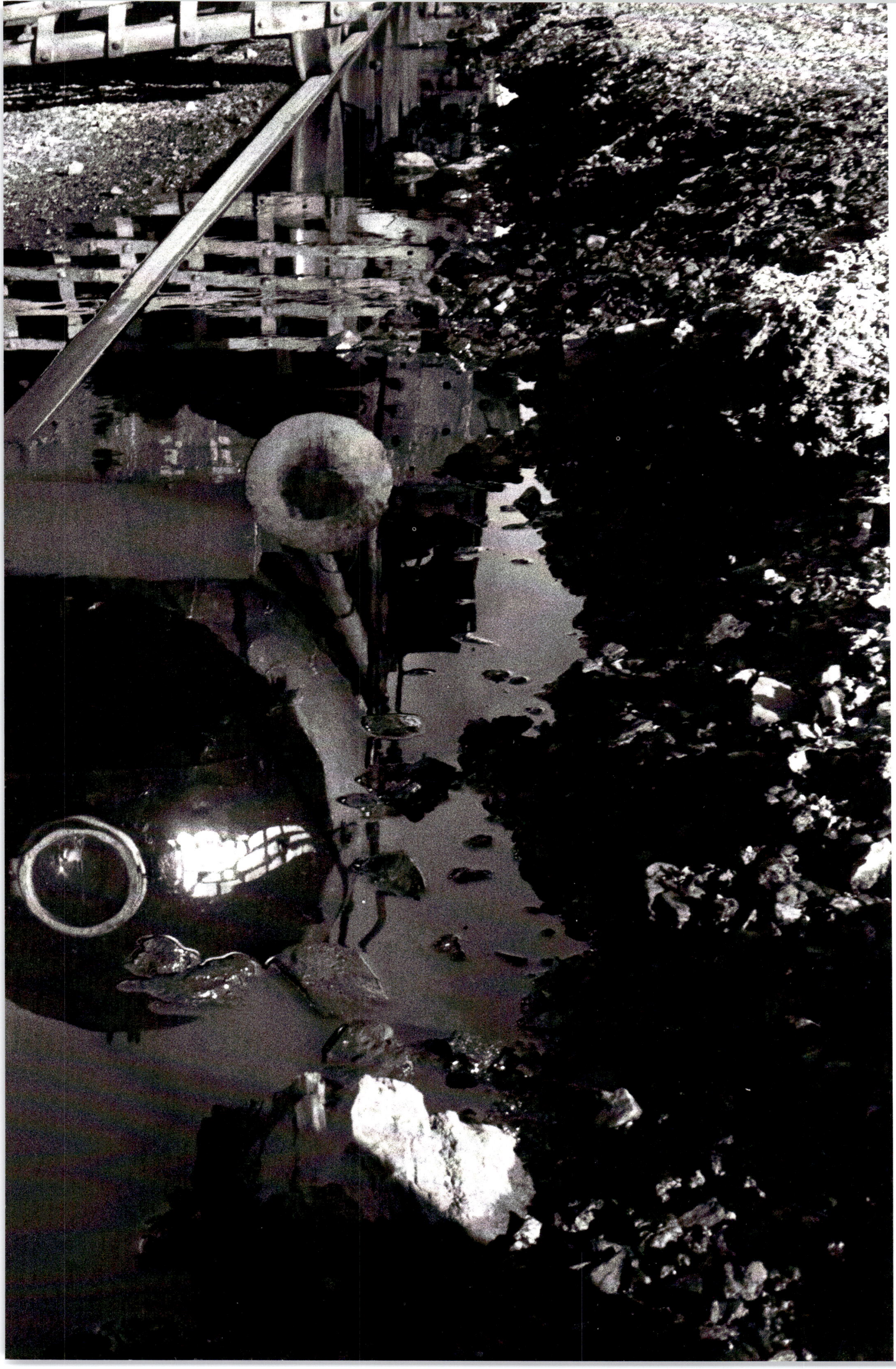

Boy with kite jumps over a puddle at Moradabad, Uttar Pradesh.

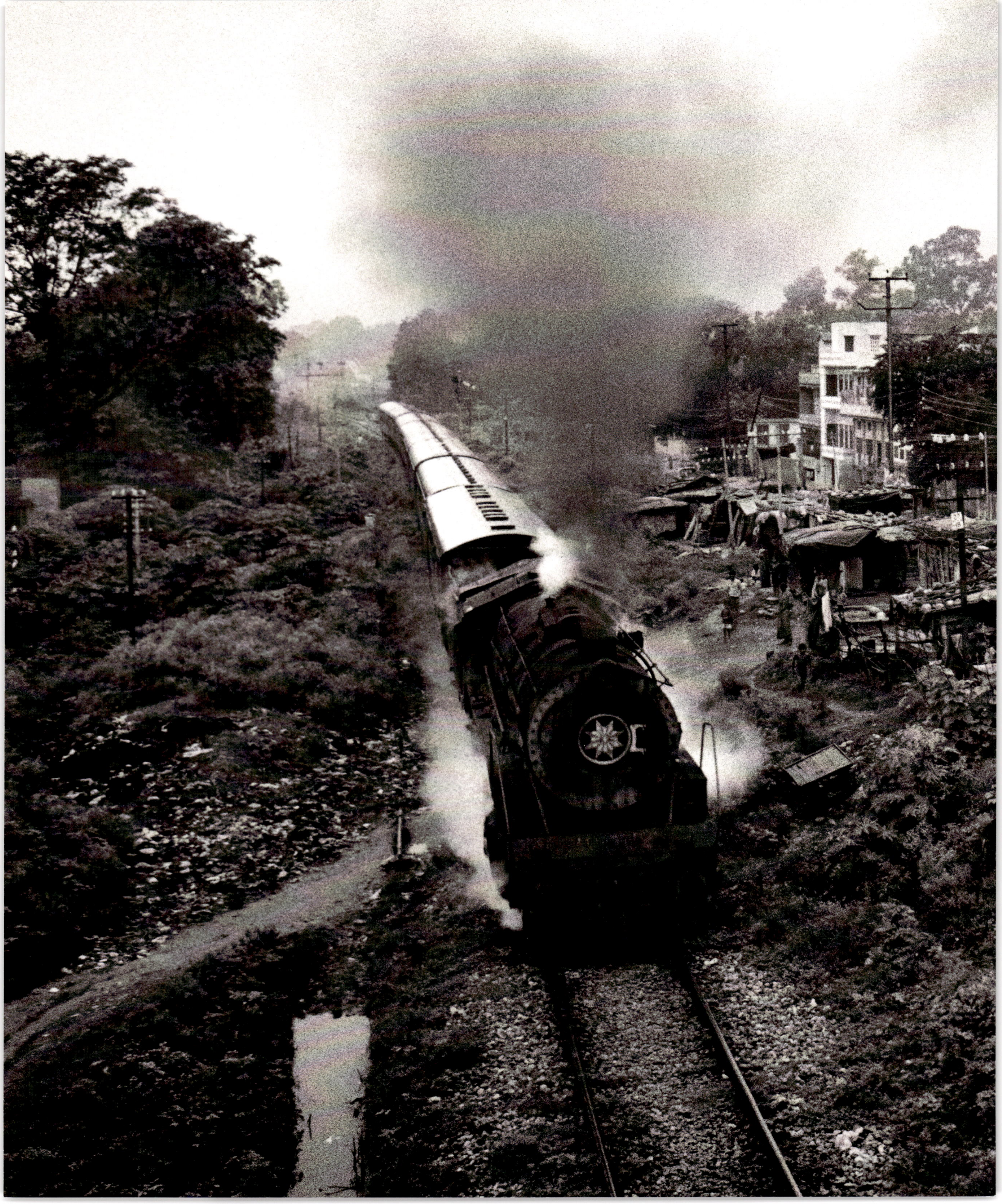

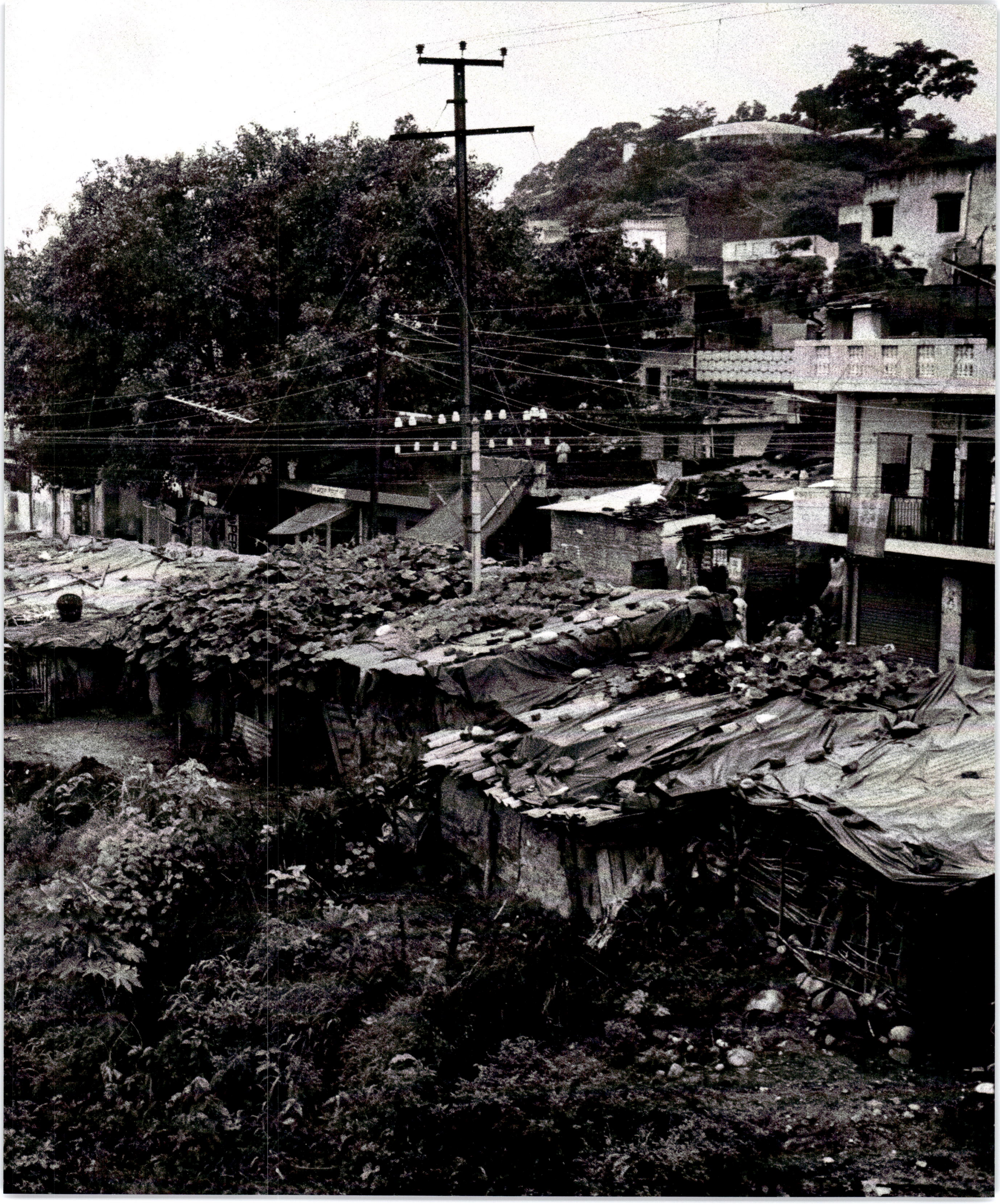

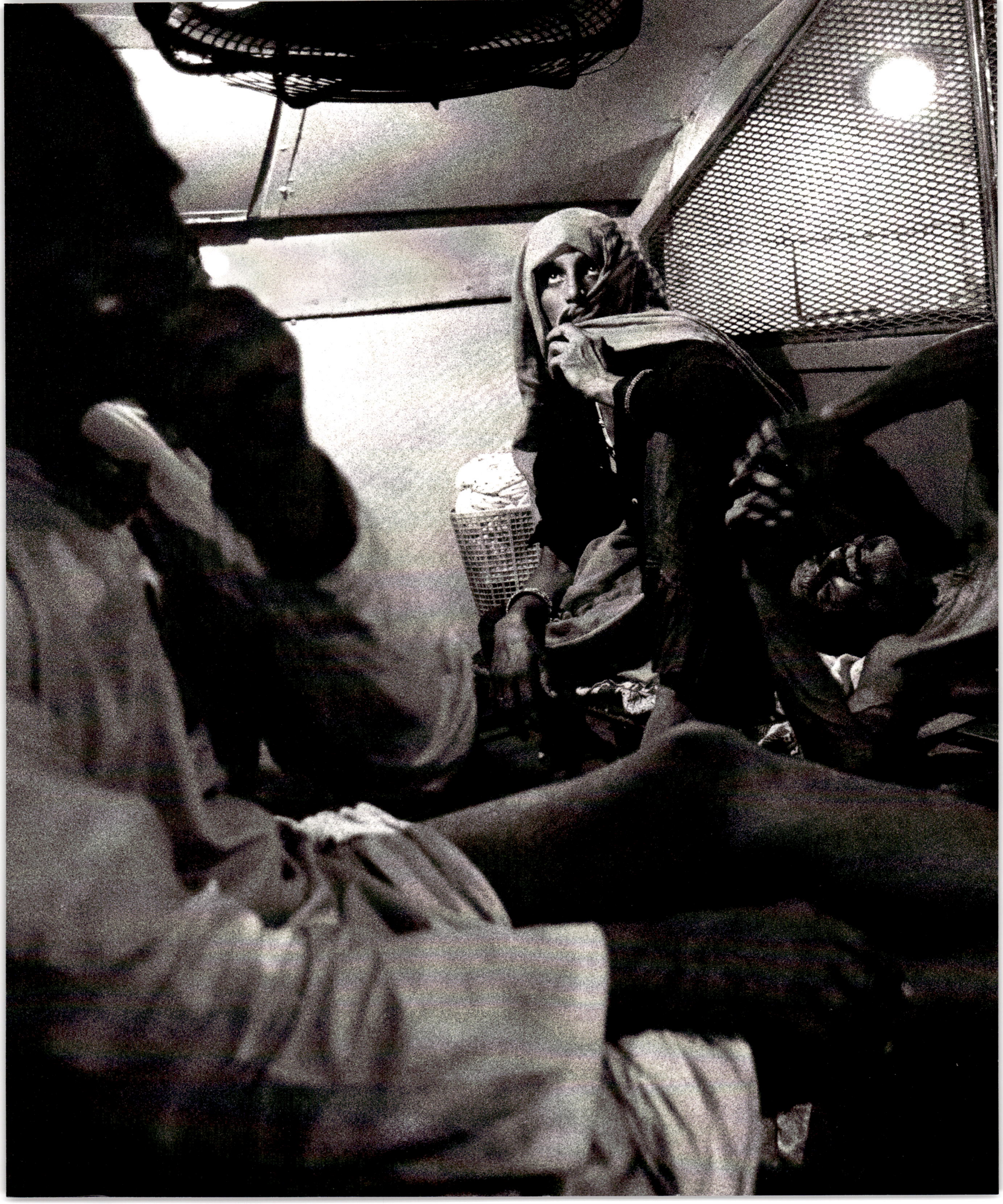

previous page
A steam train
arrives at
Haridwar from
Rishikesh.

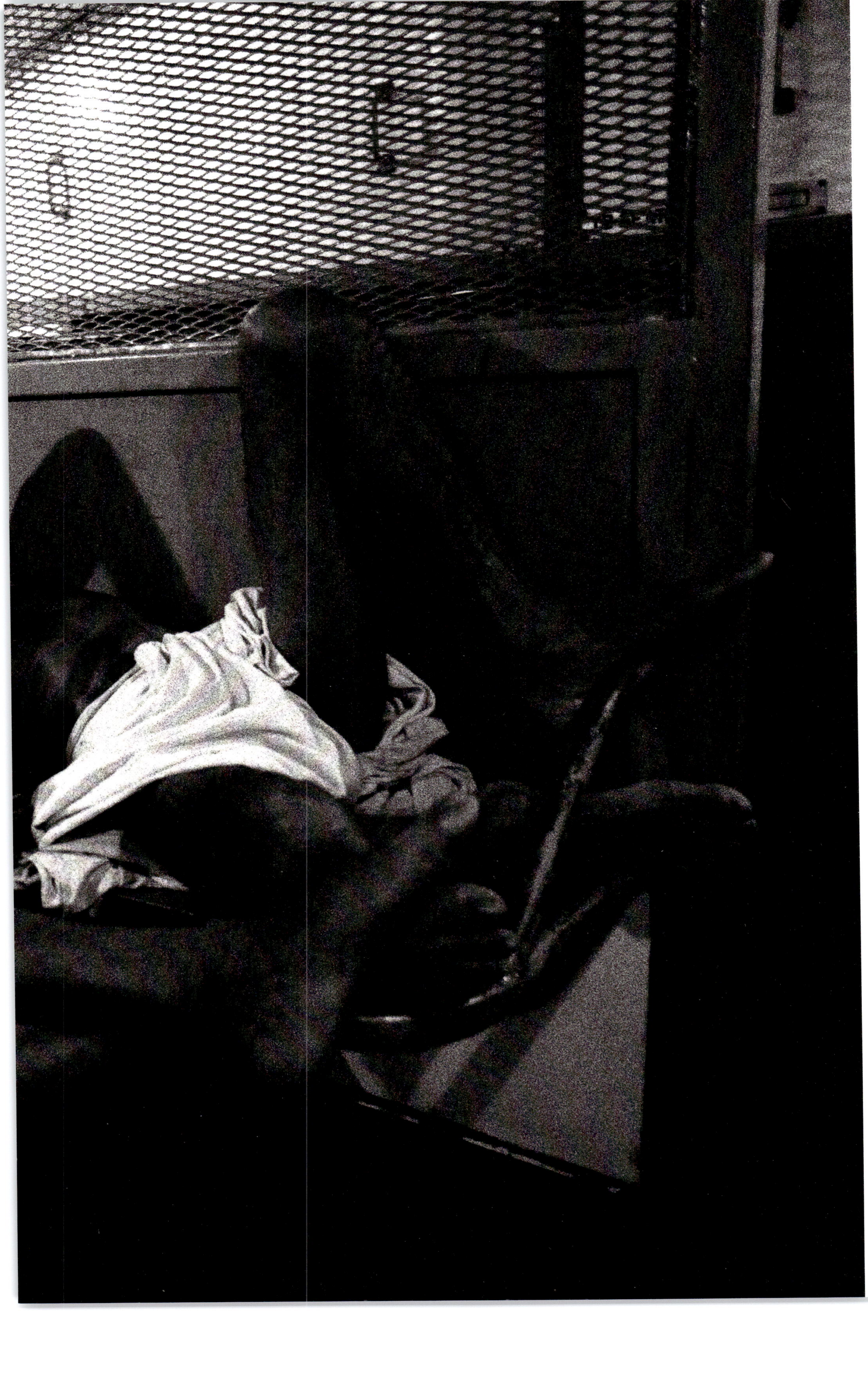

Passengers
travelling through
Uttar Pradesh.

India's most luxurious train – *the Palace on Wheels* – picks up passengers at Cantonment Station, Delhi.

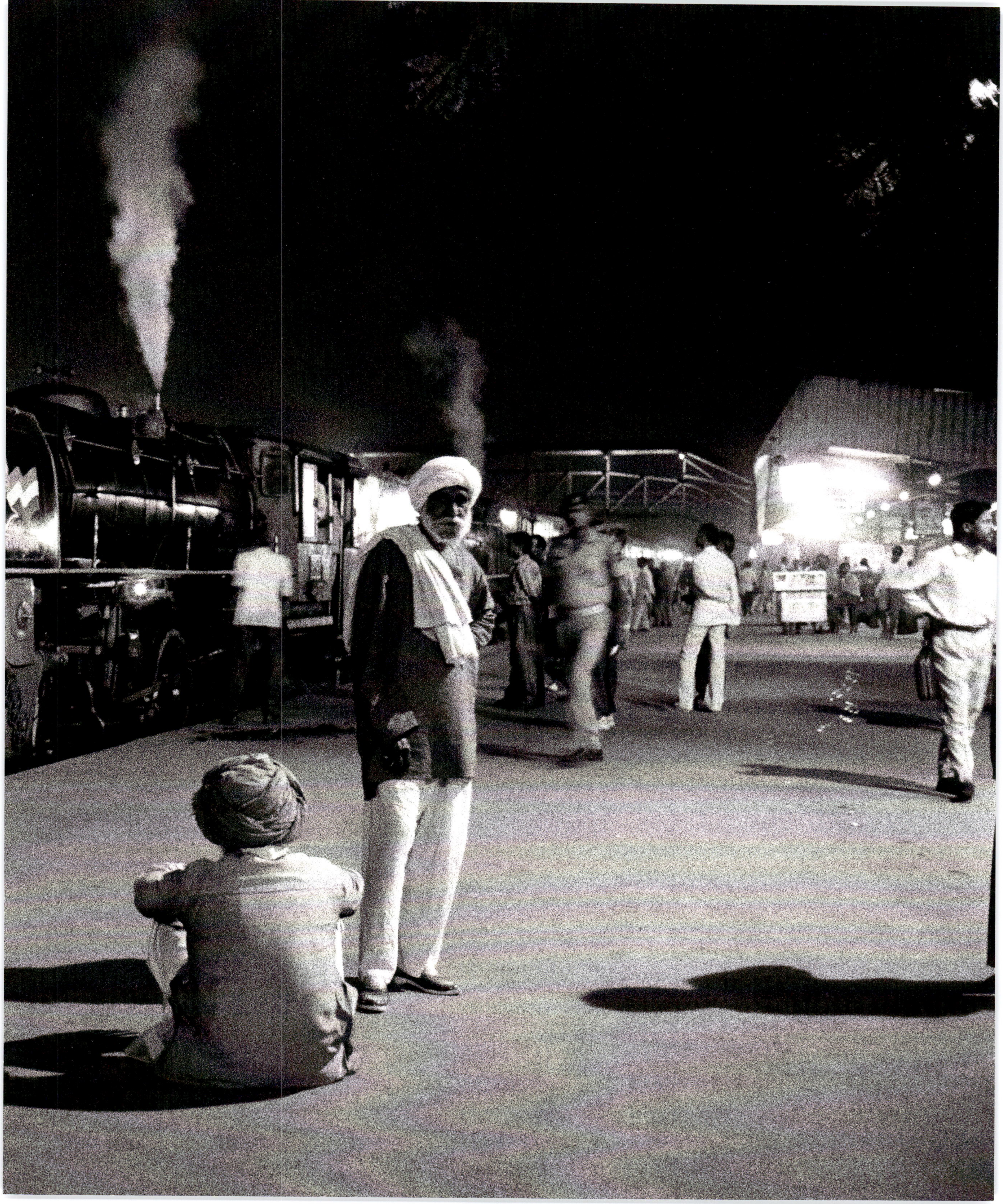

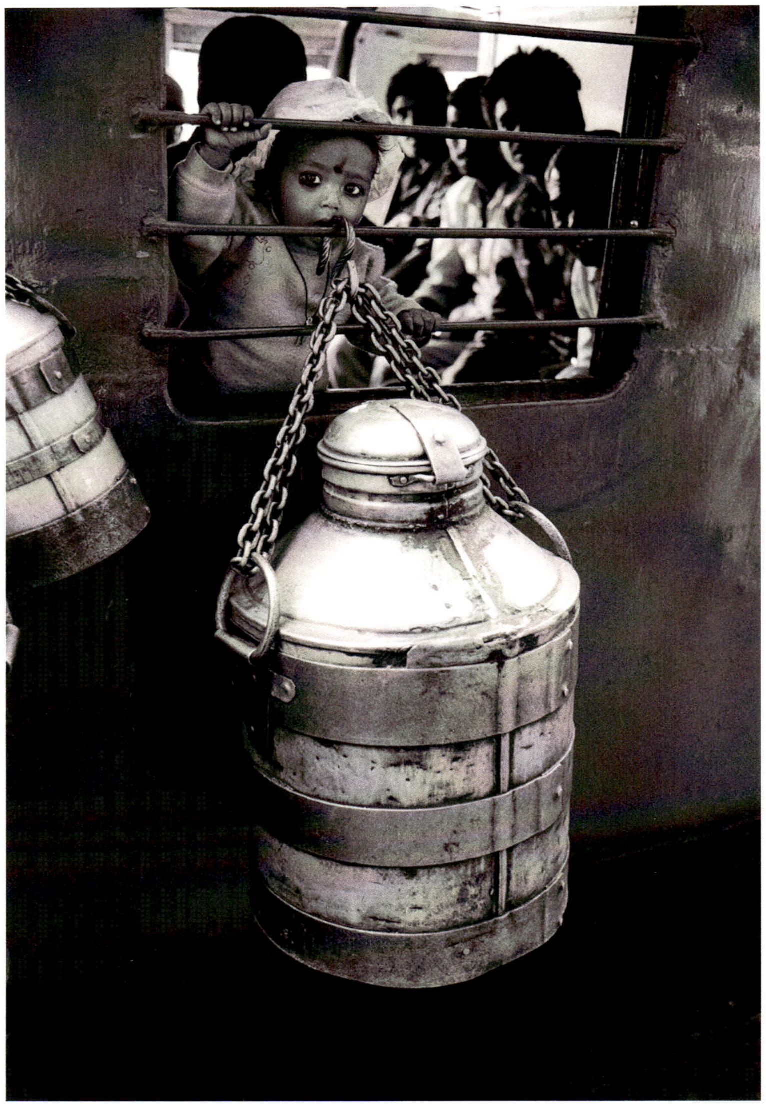

A steam train stops at Indore Station in Madhya Pradesh. Hundreds of containers of milk are transported this way from the villages to the cities.

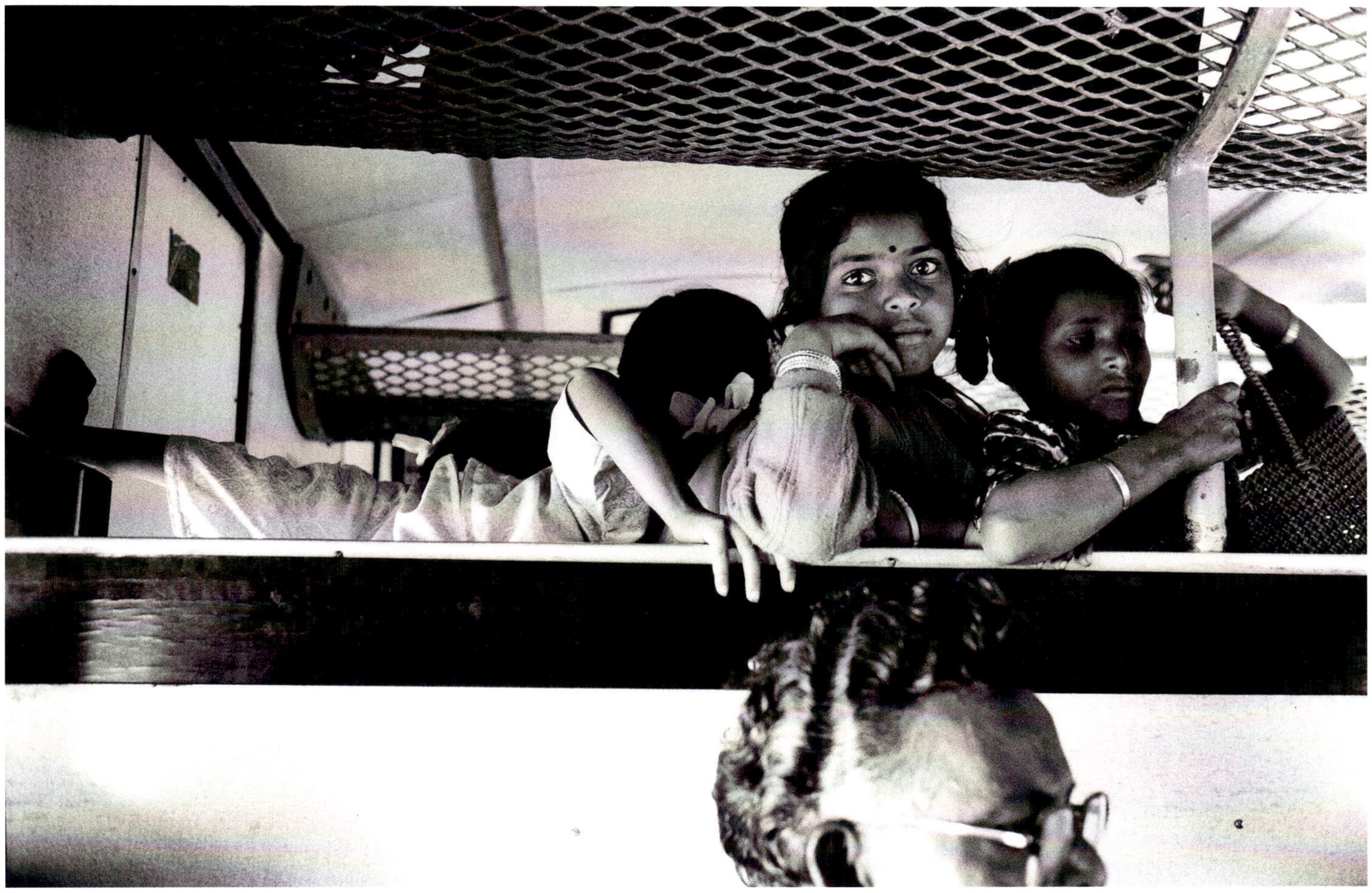

Passengers on the Nilgiri Express, Tamil Nadu.

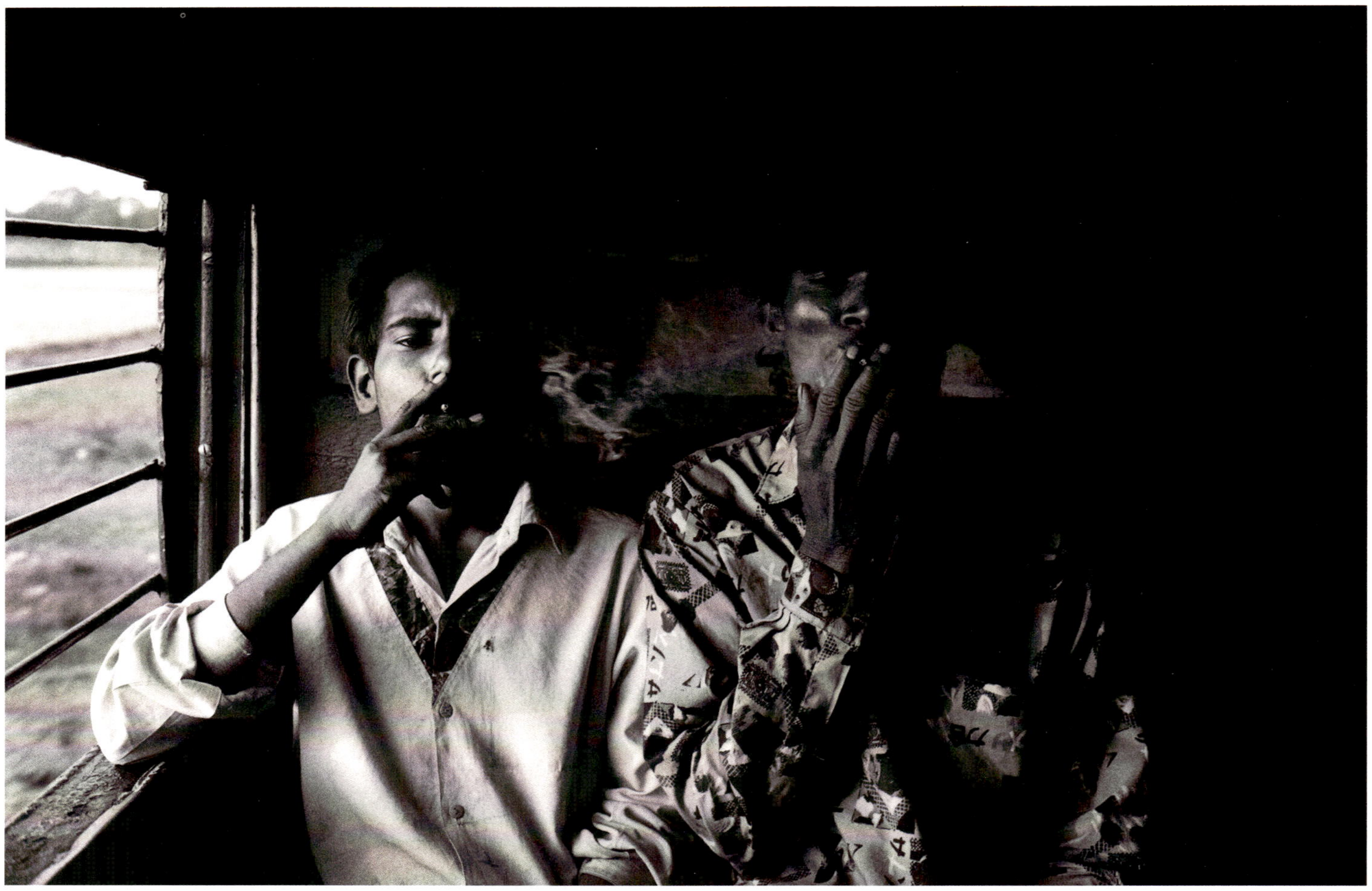

Passengers on a steam train near Indore, Madhya Pradesh.

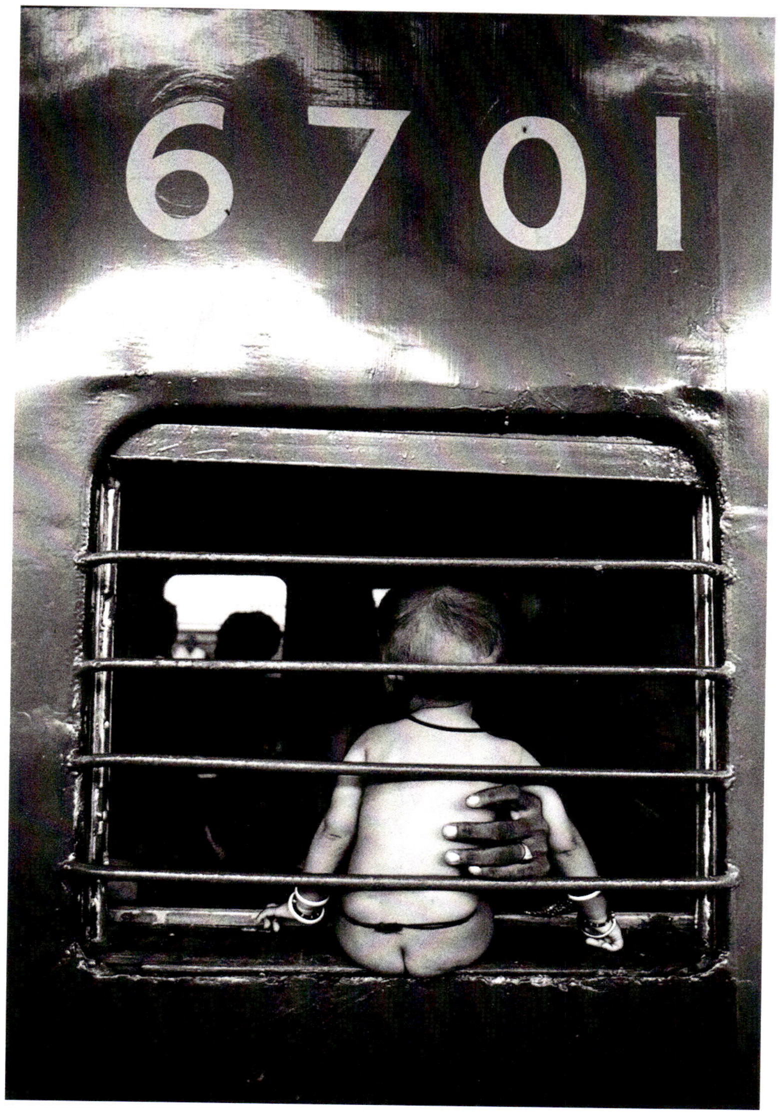

Mother and child at Saharanpur railway station.

following page
A steam train passing a farmer working in the Madhya Pradesh countryside, near Indore.

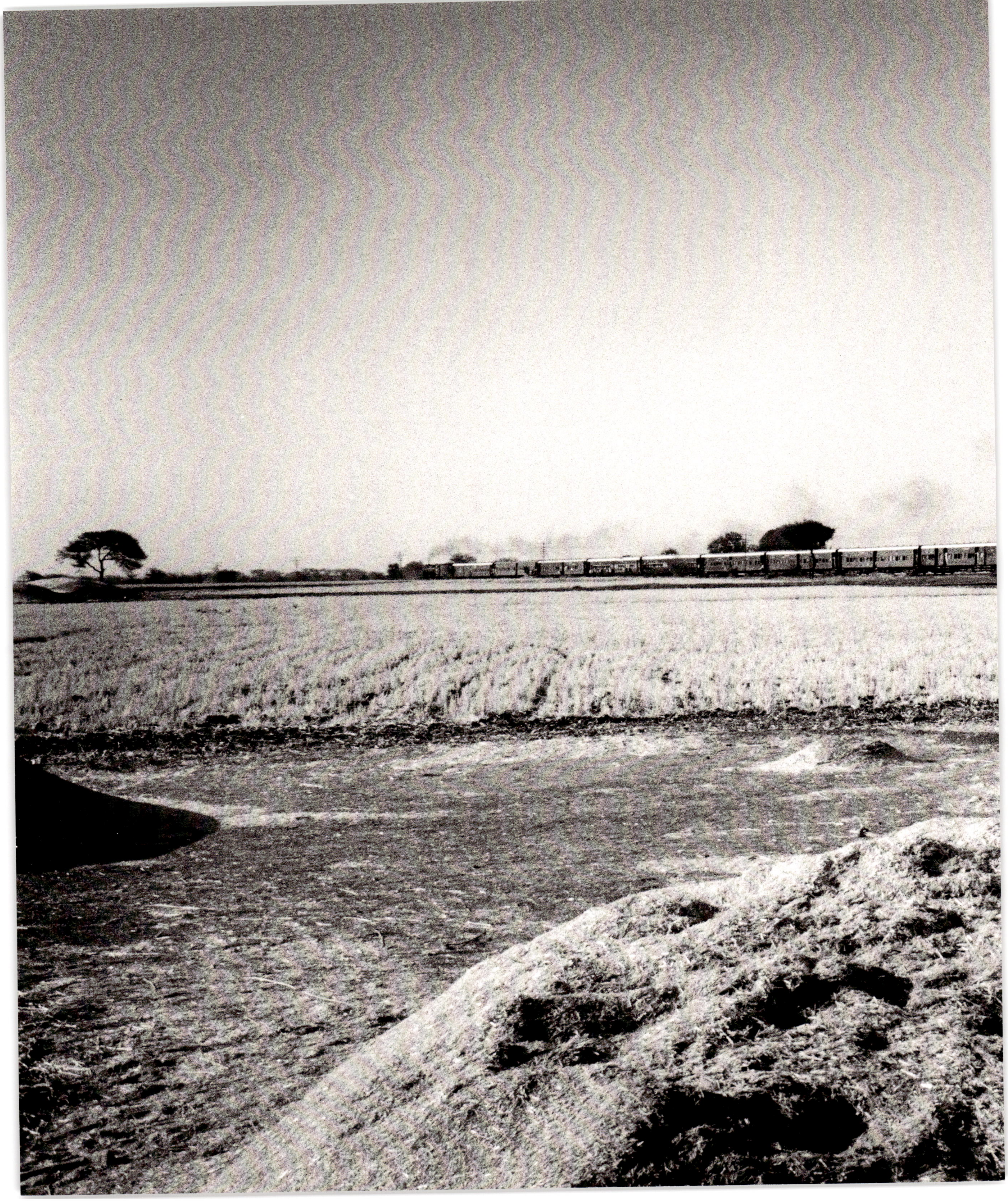

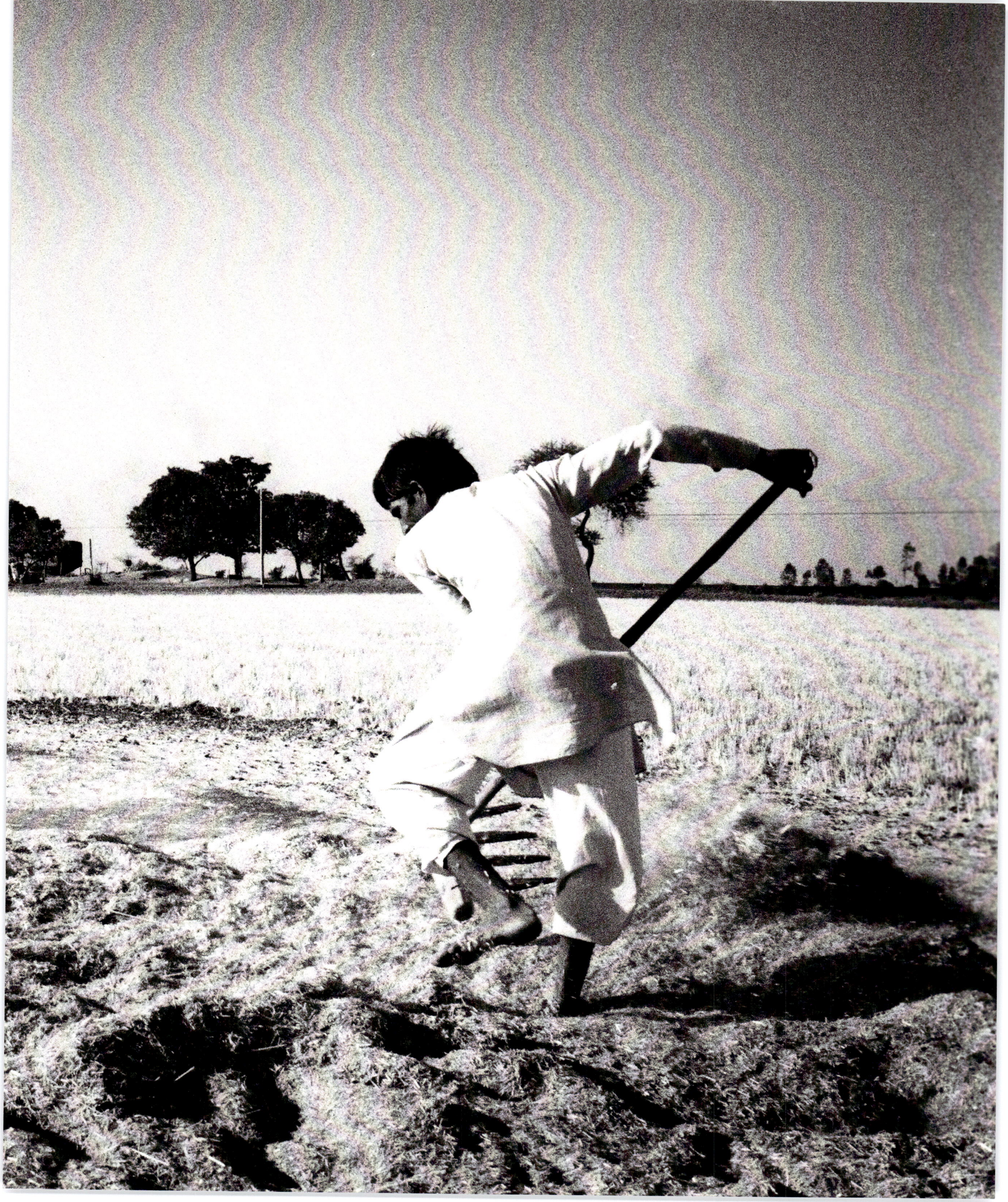

Acknowledgements

This project could never have been completed without the support and friendship of many people – many involved directly, others indirectly... my indebtedness to you all.

Firstly to my family, Stanley, Jan and Lana. To my mother who always stood by me and believed in my dreams. My love and gratitude to you all.

To Robert Pledge and the staff at Contact Press Images in Paris – Dominique, Jean-Bernard, Zara, Christophe and Corrine. To Danny Chau in London, who has printed my pictures from the beginning and always so brilliantly. To all of those in Delhi, Dieter Ludvig, Farah, Doug Curran, Tim and Jack McGirk, Padma Rao, Bhawan Singh at India Today and especially John Moore at AP. To Jean-Francois Leroy and the staff at Visa Pour L'Image; Philipp Roulet at Mise Au Point, Paris; Keith Cavanagh at the Tom Blau Gallery, London. To the many others... Marloes Krijinen at Transworld Agency, Holland; Arpedt and all the staff at World Press Photo, Amsterdam; Agathe Gaillard; Giorgia Fiorio; John Easterby at IPG, London; Neil Burgess at Network Photographers, London; Christian Caujolle; Jean-Luc Marty and Sylvie Rebbot at French Geo; Alexis Cordesse; Tom Stoddart; Marc Schlossman; Mark Sealey at Autograph, London; Michael Rand; Susan Glen and Victoria Lukens at The Independent on Sunday; Ricky Davilla Wood and Martha in Madrid; Roger Hutchings; Jean-Marie Montali at Le Figaro Magazine; Paul Blackmore; Aidan Sullivan at The Sunday Times Magazine; Patrick and Sylvie Riviere at Sydney Freelance Agency; Philip Quirk at Wildlight Photo Agency, Sydney; Stanley Greene; Boris Bencie; J.B.Avril; Joshua Haruni; Russell Shakespeare; Keith Collie and many, many more.....

To my closest friends, Jack and Alison, Ben Bohane, Paul Raffaele, Michael Amendolia, Thushara Peiris, Lucy and Eddie Monsoon, Christophe and Vanina Calais, Brendan and Lilli Beirne... my gratitude and love.

To Mark Tully, for his introduction to the book... the author I've yet to meet, but hope to soon. Your words bring the flavour of India... thank you. And to Dewi Lewis who believed in this book... my sincerest thanks.

My deepest thanks go to all the people I photographed (not just those in the book). To all those who helped along the way, who with immense generosity took me into their homes, shared meals and conversations...

And lastly... my inspiration, my love, my best friend, Jacqueline Vicario.

First published in the United Kingdom in 1999 by
Dewi Lewis Publishing, 8 Broomfield Road, Heaton Moor, Stockport SK4 4ND, England.
+44 (0)161 442 9450

All rights reserved
Copyright ©1999
For the photographs and captions: Stephen Dupont
For the introductory text: Mark Tully
For this edition: Dewi Lewis Publishing

ISBN: 1-899-235-27-2

The rights of Stephen Dupont and Mark Tully to be identified as authors of this work have been asserted by them in accordance with the Copyright, Designs and Patents Act 1988

Design and artwork production by Dewi Lewis Publishing. Printed in Italy by EBS Verona